Illicit Trade

The Illegal Wildlife Trade in Southeast Asia

INSTITUTIONAL CAPACITIES IN INDONESIA, SINGAPORE, THAILAND AND VIET NAM

Please cite this publication as:
OECD (2019), *The Illegal Wildlife Trade in Southeast Asia: Institutional Capacities in Indonesia, Singapore, Thailand and Viet Nam*, Illicit Trade, OECD Publishing, Paris, *https://doi.org/10.1787/14fe3297-en*.

ISBN 978-92-64-70887-7 (print)
ISBN 978-92-64-96712-0 (pdf)

Illicit Trade
ISSN 2617-5827 (print)
ISSN 2617-5835 (online)

Photo credits: © mr.kriangsak kitisak

Corrigenda to OECD publications may be found on line at: *www.oecd.org/about/publishing/corrigenda.htm*.

Foreword

Today, there is global recognition that poaching wildlife has a devastating impact on ecosystems and contributes to increasing corruption and financing other illegal activities. Driven by demand around the world, and using complex and sophisticated transport systems, the illegal wildlife trade touches nearly every country in the world. While its impacts are felt most acutely at local level, the stakes are global and the solutions require international co-operation.

The Sustainable Development Goals (SDG) call on countries to take urgent action to end poaching and trafficking of species. Yet many countries are struggling to make progress on this front. According to the latest SDG progress report, in 2018 over 7,000 species continue to be trafficked illegally in the world in over 120 countries. Collective efforts to combat this form of illicit trade need to be accelerated now.

This report examines institutional gaps that affect the capacity of governments to address the illegal wildlife trade in Southeast Asia. Wildlife crime is "low-risk, high-reward", making it particularly attractive to criminal networks that exploit weaknesses in governance systems to help acquire, transport and sell illegal wildlife. The wide range of institutions and government officials who are targeted and at risk of being corrupted underscores the need for urgent, comprehensive and coordinated action across the public administrations of the countries concerned.

Building on an analysis of the illegal wildlife trade in East Africa by OECD in 2018, this report provides a regional focus on Southeast Asia, drawing on research conducted in Indonesia, Singapore, Thailand and Vietnam. It aims to increase the understanding of institutional vulnerabilities that are continually exploited in the conduct of the illegal wildlife trade in Southeast Asia.

The report identifies good practices that could be replicated to tackle wildlife crime effectively through law enforcement and reinforced legislative and regulatory frameworks. Its recommendations propose concrete actions for donor agencies, law enforcement bodies, international organisations and NGOs to take to improve actions in the fight against the illegal wildlife trade. These recommendations concern key issues such as the need for national strategies to combat illicit trade, how to improve inter-agency coordination and the need to strengthen co-operation and information sharing across countries in the region and beyond.

The study was conducted in the Public Governance Directorate by the Secretariat of the OECD Task Force on Countering Illicit Trade (TF-CIT). The study benefitted from over 90 field interviews in Indonesia, Singapore, Thailand and Viet Nam, as well as findings generated from research and global seizure data from World Customs Organisation and TRAFFIC databases, complemented by extensive desk-based research.

Acknowledgments

The Illegal Wildlife Trade in Southeast Asia report was prepared by the OECD Directorate for Public Governance (GOV), under the overall guidance of Marcos Bonturi, Director.

The review was produced by the OECD Reform of Public Sector Division (GOV/RPS). Michael Morantz prepared and drafted the report, under the supervision of Jack Radisch. Rob Parry Jones (WWF), Josie Raine (Freeland), Nichanan Tanthanawit (Freeland) and Sallie Yang (USAID/Freeland) made important contributions.

As cited throughout, the report draws extensively on analysis carried out by public officials and NGOs that combat illegal wildlife trade in Indonesia, Singapore, Thailand and Viet Nam.

We are also grateful to Brian Gillikin for providing research support and quantitative analysis and to Liv Gaunt, Raquel Páramo and Javier González for valuable editorial and administrative assistance.

Acronyms and abbreviations

ACRES	Animal Concerns Research and Education Society
AGO	Indonesia Attorney General's Office
AMLO	Thailand Anti-Money Laundering Offices
AEG	ASEAN Experts Group on CITES
ASEAN	Association of Southeast Asian Nations
ASEAN-WEN	ASEAN Wildlife Enforcement Network
ASEAN SOMTC	ASEAN Senior Officials Meeting on Transnational Crime
APG	Asia Pacific Group on Anti-Money Laundering
AVA	Singapore Agri-Food and Veterinary Authority
CBD	the Convention on Biological Diversity
CITES	the Convention on International Trade in Endangered Species of Wild Fauna and Flora
CMAA	Customs Mutual Assistance Agreement
CPIB	Singapore Corrupt Practices Investigation Bureau
DNP	Thailand Department of National Parks, Wildlife and Plant Conservation
ENV	Education for Nature Viet Nam
FATF	Financial Action Task Force
FIU	Financial Intelligence Unit
FTZ	Free Trade Zone

GI-AGB	Viet Nam Government Inspectorate Anti-Corruption Bureau
ICA	Singapore Immigration and Checkpoints Authority
ICCWC	the International Consortium on Combating Wildlife Crime
INTERPOL	the International Criminal Police Organization
KPK	Indonesia Corruption Eradication Commission
MARD	Viet Nam Ministry of Agriculture and Rural Development
MLAT	Mutual Legal Assistance Treaty
MNRE	Thailand Ministry of Natural Resources and Environment
MPS	Viet Nam Ministry of Public Safety
NACC	Thailand National Anti-Corruption Commission
NCB	INTERPOL National Contact Bureau
NEST	INTERPOL National Environmental Security Task Force
NIAP	Thailand National Ivory Action Plan
NSCA	Viet Nam National Steering Committee on Anti-Corruption
NRECD	Royal Thai Police, Natural Resources and Environmental Crime Suppression Division
OAG	Indonesia Office of the Attorney General
OECD	Organisation for Economic Co-operation and Development
PPATK	Indonesia Financial Transaction Reports and Analysis Centre
SCA	Singapore Customs Authority
SDG	United Nations Sustainable Development Goals

SPP	Viet Nam Supreme Peoples' Procuracy
TI	Transparency International
UNDP	United Nations Development Programme
UNODC	United Nations Office of Drugs and Crime
UNTOC	United Nations Convention against Transnational Organized Crime
WARPA	Thailand Wild Animal Reservation and Protection Act, 1992
WEN	Wildlife Enforcement Network
WCS WCU	Wildlife Conservation Society Wildlife Crimes Unit
WWF	World Wildlife Fund

Table of Contents

Tables

Figures

Boxes

Executive Summary

Illicit trade generates billions of dollars annually for transnational criminal networks. Among the most sinister and most profitable forms of illicit trade is the illegal wildlife trade. The illegal wildlife trade is more than just an ecological issue; it can have significant economic impacts by creating disruptive imbalances in ecosystems for sustainable growth, and more directly on eco-tourism markets. Wildlife crime is such an ominous challenge that its reduction is designated as a target in the Sustainable Development Goals.

This report focuses on the illegal wildlife trade in Southeast Asia, where extensive poaching occurs on a commercial scale and natural resources are ravaged for short-term profits. These countries also serve as transit points and destination markets for wildlife and wildlife products that have been shipped across illicit global supply chains. In the coming years, hundreds of species in Southeast Asia are projected to go extinct. Governments must take stronger actions to tackle this form of illicit trade through concerted regional co-operation.

Long-term strategies to sensitize the public to the value of protecting natural resources and national heritage are important components of a holistic approach to combatting this form of trade. Unfortunately, the pace at which certain populations are dwindling, e.g. the pangolin, requires more urgent measures. The commitment and capacity of law enforcement in many countries is key to ensure sufficient wildlife populations for the longer-term strategies to be remain relevant.

This report focuses on the institutional capacities of law enforcement to combat the illegal wildlife trade in Indonesia, Singapore, Thailand and Viet Nam. In recent years, these four Southeast Asian countries have been at the centre of the illegal wildlife trade debate concerning enforcement of wildlife crimes. Do legislative loopholes restrict effective enforcement to the protection of domestic species only? Is law enforcement co-ordination across administrations and across borders progressing or standing-still while the march toward extinction of species continues? This report gathered information from field research in these four Southeast Asian countries, and considers what further reforms could lead to better law enforcement outcomes.

Illicit trade is motivated by profit and wildlife crime is low risk and high reward. Controls can fail at multiple points in the trade chain leading to ineffective institutional responses. Corruption at maritime ports, airports and at land border crossings provide channels for the entry of a range of illicit products. Legal gaps and loopholes and un-enforceable provisions of laws permit the sale of illegal wildlife products. Traffickers operate with impunity in some public marketplaces. Proceeds of wildlife crime flow across borders and raise questions about the financial integrity of certain banks.

The report offers regional insights into the causes and consequences of this global challenge. It presents a broad overview of the key institutional frameworks and distils the key findings into policy prescriptions that should increase the effectiveness of law enforcement agencies responsible for combatting wildlife crime.

The key findings:

- Southeast Asian countries are source, transit and destination markets for illegal wildlife trade. Traffickers do not discriminate between domestic and foreign wildlife species, which are shipped and consumed throughout the region.
- Inter-agency co-operation is recognized as a key to successful law enforcement efforts but the number of cases involving inter-agency co-operation for illegal wildlife trade investigations and prosecutions is low. Several countries have adopted 'wildlife enforcement networks' (WENs), yet few of these inter-agency frameworks are shown to be operationally active on a regular or pro-active basis. Furthermore, anti-corruption authorities and financial intelligence units are included in WENs in only half of the countries studied.
- International co-operation actions in the form of legal information sharing agreements, extradition treaties and global wildlife task forces have gained strength in recent years. Nevertheless, the ties between Southeast Asian countries and authorities in different, source and transit regions remain underdeveloped.
- Legal loopholes and gaps in implementation of laws continue to prevent effective prosecution of illegal wildlife trade. Illegal wildlife products can be licensed for export or sale through captive breeding programs or in open markets, often masquerading as legally obtained products.
- Corruption risks are facilitators of wildlife trade in several of the countries studied. National border crossings are hot spots for corruption.
- There is currently no effective system in place to tackle the illicit financial flows from wildlife trafficking sales. The majority of FIUs have not participated in investigations related to the laundering of proceeds of wildlife crime.

The recommendations:

The OECD Task Force on Countering Illicit Trade stands ready to support governments in adopting robust governance frameworks to counter the illegal wildlife trade, and to implement the key recommendations below. OECD standards and analysis may provide useful tools for this purpose, including: the OECD Recommendations of the Council on Public Integrity, the OECD Declaration on Public Sector Innovation, as well as Best Practices for Performance Budgeting in Government.

Based on the key findings above, countries should develop a national strategy on countering the illegal wildlife trade, and budget sufficient resources to monitor the implementation of actions it calls for.

- Governments should convene a Task Force that brings together relevant administrations (including police, customs, officers of the criminal courts, CITES enforcement agencies, and financial intelligence units) to design a national strategy.
- The national strategy should:
  - Reflect commitments under relevant international conventions such as CITES, the United Nations Convention against Transnational Organized Crime, the United Nations Convention against Corruption, and reflects relevant targets of the SDGs.
  - Incorporate the findings from a legislative and capacity gap analysis to address shortfalls in existing laws, or enforceability gaps of law enforcement.

- Include policy dialogues with central government administrations including participation at the ministerial level elevate the costs of illegal wildlife and benefits of mitigation measures for long-term economic and ecological prosperity.
- Strengthen co-operation between law enforcement and wildlife conservations authorities, through the drafting of strategic objectives and joint-investigations.
- Take into account the G20 High Level Principles on Combatting Corruption Related to Illegal Trade in Wildlife and Wildlife Products and call for the conduct of anti-corruption investigations by police and anti-corruption authorities on the back of arrests for wildlife crimes to identify and prosecute related criminal networks.
- Reinforce the engagement of financial intelligence units in follow-the-money investigations related to wildlife crime, both at national level and in co-operation with international partners.
- Foster international co-ordination and operations with relevant counterparts.

1 Introduction

The chapter introduces the topic of illegal wildlife trade in the Southeast Asia, providing the purpose and methodology of this report.

Southeast Asia plays an important source and gateway role in the global illegal wildlife trade. Association of Southeast Asian Nations (ASEAN)[1] countries account for under 3% of the world's land mass and 8% of the global population, but the region is estimated to account for 25% of the global illegal wildlife trade (Lin, 2005[1]). Within the region, illegally traded wildlife is consumed, transhipped, processed, refined and sold. Open marketplaces for illegal wildlife continue to flourish due to gaps in regulations, legal loopholes, smuggling and corruption. Southeast Asia is also an entryway to China, the world's largest consumer market for illegal wildlife products, and other consumer countries in Asia including Japan (UNODC, 2013[2]).

Criminal networks are at the heart of the illegal wildlife trade throughout the region. Using highly developed trade infrastructure and strong integration into the global economy. Organized criminal groups leverage loosely affiliated networks of familial ties, corrupt officials and intimidation of publicly registered companies to buy, sell, poach and export illegal wildlife without detection. They may use major airports and seaports as hubs for globally sourced illegal wildlife from Africa, Europe and the Americas, but also smaller and more disperse landing spots. The borders of countries with many islands are difficult to monitor and control, which facilitates transit of both domestic and internationally sourced illegal wildlife and wildlife products. Proceeds of wildlife crimes flow through the global financial system, with profits placed and layered into the bank accounts and properties of criminal enterprises, often with the intention of re-financing the next hunt, bribe or transport arrangement of endangered species.

There is broad consensus among the international community of the negative effects of the illegal wildlife trade and that efforts to combat smuggling, trade fraud, corruption and money laundering are key measures that governments could enact to limit or deter these crimes. After decades of increases in poaching, habitat loss and illegal consumption, many species are threatened with extinction. Public awareness of the plight of iconic species such as the African Elephant and the Black Rhino is relatively high, yet numerous Asian species are also prey to illegal wildlife markets. In Southeast Asia, the Asian Elephant population has declined by 50% over the past century. The four species of Asian pangolins are now among most poached animals in the world[2] (Jani Actman, 2016[3]). Southeast Asian birds such as the helmeted hornbill are now listed as critically endangered due to the popularity of their carved skulls (National Geographic, 2018[4]). Among Asian rhinos, the Sumatra and Java are critically endangered, numbering fewer than 80 and 70 in the wild, respectively (WWF, 2019[5]).

Illegal wildlife trade is inherently unsustainable. The illegal taking, killing and trading in endangered species damages biodiversity, which in turn affects the prospects of long-term, sustainable economic development. The commercial-scale depletion of ecosystems is likely to create long-term pressure on agricultural outputs, forestry practises, and food security. According to the UN Intergovernmental Science-Policy Platform on Biodiversity and Ecosystem Services (IPBES) report, "biodiversity and ecosystem functions and services, are deteriorating worldwide", posing a long-term threat to humanity's wellbeing (IPBES, 2019[6]) .

The illegal sale of wildlife products fuels a multi-billion dollar criminal market (UNODC, 2014[7]). In Southeast Asia, networks of opportunistic actors are involved in multi-tonne, multi-million dollar shipments of illegal wildlife trade products, many of which are sourced in, transit through, or consumed within the focus countries in this report. Criminal enterprises use bribery and intimidation, complex logistics structures and networks of criminal actors to ensure that goods make their way to points of sale. Proceeds of crime derived from illegal wildlife trade is laundered into the global financial system. Throughout the region, these actions undermine the rule of law, and affect access to justice and integrity of public sectors.

The United Nations Sustainable Development Goals (SDGs) recognize poaching and trafficking as a global risk. SDG Target 15.7 urges countries to "Take urgent action to end poaching and trafficking of protected species of flora and fauna and address both demand and supply of illegal wildlife products" (UN, 2018[8]). The indicator for SDG 15.7 is the "Proportion of traded wildlife that was poached or illicitly trafficked", meaning that the immediate objective of this SDG is to see a net reduction of the scale of illegal wildlife products and live specimens to directly address this pressing challenge. SDG 16, seeks to "promote peaceful and inclusive societies for sustainable development, provide access to justice for all and build effective, accountable and inclusive institutions at all levels" (UN, 2018[8]). Illegal wildlife trade (IWT) prevents the achievement of several goals and targets under SDG 16, namely the reduction in illicit financial flows (SDG 16.4); the reduction of corruption and bribery (16.5); effective and transparent institutions (16.6) and more broadly speaking, rule of law at the national and international levels (SDG 16.3) (UN, 2018[8]).

Southeast Asia should be a high priority region for international efforts to address the illegal wildlife trade. It is a hotspot for the sale and consumption of illegal wildlife for hundreds of domestic endangered species such as the tiger, the Sumatran orangutan, the helmeted hornbill bird and the Sumatran rhino, which are on the path to extinction in the wild. Despite this, discussions on reduction of the illegal wildlife trade, particularly in the international arena, often focus on the reduction of poaching and trafficking across source and transit countries in sub-Saharan Africa. Meanwhile, there is relatively less global attention paid to the dynamics, drivers and institutional gaps that facilitate Southeast Asian marketplaces and reinforce the networks between sources in Africa and consumption in Asia.

This report details the findings of research conducted throughout 2018, documenting evidence collected from field interviews, desk research and data collection on institutional capacities to counter illegal wildlife trade. This study focused on four countries: Indonesia, Singapore, Thailand and Viet Nam. The OECD undertook this project to further increase global action against this "low-risk, high reward" (OECD, 2016[9]) crime with the aim to enhance awareness of the risks, facilitators and gaps that enable illegal wildlife trade in the region. The analysis in this report lead to recommendations on tackling specific enablers of wildlife crime, including corruption, money laundering, and gaps in legislation and enforcement.

This OECD report is the second of a series on illicit trade focusing on the illegal wildlife trade. In 2018, the OECD published "*Strengthening Governance and Reducing Corruption Risks to Tackle Illegal Wildlife Trade: Lessons from East and Southern Africa*". The first report drew lessons from country studies conducted in Kenya, Tanzania, Uganda and Zambia. Building upon the findings of this first phase of research, the current report similarly presents an assessment and recommendations to reduce or deter the illegal wildlife trade in the Southeast Asia region.

The report also builds on previous OECD work conducted under the auspices of the Task Force on Countering Illicit Trade (TF-CIT), which has served as a platform for countries to share experience on combatting all forms of illicit trade, including the illegal wildlife trade. The 2016 OECD report 'Illicit Trade: Converging Criminal Networks' presented a dedicated chapter on illegal wildlife trade, focusing on trafficking trends in sub-Saharan Africa, outlining key hot spots and hubs for illegal trafficking flows (OECD, 2016[9]). For the research and analysis on corruption, this report draws upon the work of the OECD Integrity Forum, which held a specific session on illegal wildlife trade in 2016 and 2017. Most recently, the 2018 OECD report 'Governance Frameworks to Counter Illicit Trade' highlighted the institutional gaps facing governments in efforts to penalise illicit trade, with a dedicated study of illegal wildlife trade and the penalties, sanctions and national strategies of governments to address it. In an overview of select economies, it found that such crimes are typically penalised through relatively light sentences, with little pursuit of charges for associated crimes, like corruption or money laundering (OECD, 2018[10]).

As highlighted in the recommendations of this report, the scourge of illegal wildlife trade in Southeast Asia calls for stronger support from the international community to respond to an international crisis. This means stronger support for centres of government and for governance. The OECD is well placed to take this work forward thanks its extensive policy and knowledge community. For example, the OECD offers practical support to strengthen the public governance practices that are pre-requisites for effective SDG implementation (OECD, 2019[11]). The OECD's Observatory on Public Sector Innovation can be mobilized towards the achievement of increased efficiency and effectiveness of processes to adapt and innovate in response to intractable challenges (OECD, 2019[11]). The OECD Best Practices for Performance Budgeting highlights another area where governments can benefit from OECD's toolkits for managing and maintaining efficient budgets tied to outcomes (OECD, 2019[12]). Finally, the OECD's range of work on anti-corruption in the public sector, namely the OECD Recommendation on Public Integrity, can offer tailored approaches to analysing and addressing corruption risks facing competent authorities, offering strategic and sustainable response to corruption and integrity (OECD, 2019[13]).

Purpose of the report

The aim of this report is to provide a clearer understanding of the state of play and enabling dynamics of illegal wildlife trade in Southeast Asia, and to identify the gaps in institutional capacities that enable wildlife crime to persist within Indonesia, Singapore, Thailand and Viet Nam. It offers a snapshot of wildlife crime and the institutional responses to illegal wildlife trade in the four focus countries, provides a structured overview of how each country approaches this challenge, and draws common lessons from their experiences. The report highlights key areas of vulnerability at the end of the illegal wildlife trade supply chain as the products make their way to end-users.

This report is one of only a few that has looked closely at illegal wildlife trade in Southeast Asia, and among even fewer that addresses issues such as the institutional responses to corruption risks and money laundering. The comprehensive approach adopted within this report also reflects the governance issues of concern to the OECD Public Governance Committee, reflecting the spirit of the OECD Recommendation on Public Integrity. The focus of the report on institutional and governance aspects aligns with the broader mandate of the OECD, in the public governance arena, to provide support and recommendations on governance and implementation gaps.

This report and the analysis herein is directed primarily towards governments to strengthen institutional capacities to counter illegal wildlife trade, corruption risks and illicit financial flows. The findings will be useful to a number of government agencies and administrations, including CITES Management Authorities, National Police, Customs, Financial Intelligence Units and Anti-Corruption Agencies (many of which have been interviewed and studied in this report). The recommendations contained in this report are also useful to non-governmental organisations who implement donor programming and substantive support to governments, as well as donor agencies for future illegal wildlife trade programming, strategic reviews and capacity building for joint-responses to common threats.

The findings of this report complement findings from existing initiatives to deepen the understanding of the illegal wildlife trade. Policymakers, NGOs, intergovernmental organisations and the wider academic audience are encouraged to discuss these recommendations in international fora and to apply these recommendations in response to the risks present in relation to illegal wildlife trade.

Methodology

The OECD has relied upon a select group of respondents and experts to review the methodology and findings in an effort to ensure that lessons from anonymised cases remain reflected in this report, and to ensure that the reporting on these and other sources are accurate.

Definitions

The Convention on International Trade in Endangered Species of Wild Fauna and Flora (CITES) provides the international legal basis for signatory parties to regulate trade in wildlife in a common manner. Implementation of CITES in national legislation, however, varies among signatories. As such, trade in a certain species can be legal in one country and illegal under CITES – or, by contrast, prohibited under national law and permitted under CITES. Consequently, the international community lacks a universally accepted definition of illegal wildlife trade, and interpretations of the scope vary[3].

For clarity the report adopts a clear definition of illegal wildlife trade as trade in wildlife or wildlife parts that violates either international legal frameworks or the legislation of one or several of the countries through which a wildlife product has passed. This definition thereby encompasses both domestic laws and CITES regulations. From this perspective, the term illegal wildlife trade is conceived more narrowly than 'wildlife crime', excluding illegal grazing and encroachment, among other criminal activities. It focuses on the illegal taking or trade in wild species of flora and fauna, which excludes illegal fishing and logging.

Semi-Structured Interviews

The OECD research team carried out 40 semi-structured interviews in 2018 with 94 individuals across the four focus countries. Interviews occurred primarily in face-to-face meetings in the Southeast Asian countries. Interviews engaged government officials (42%), non-governmental organisation (NGO) and independent conservation, anti-poaching and -trafficking practitioners (20%), experts based in foreign delegations (17%), experts within international organizations (13%), and independent experts (8%). Government agencies interviewed included:

- CITES management authorities (inclusive of wildlife management and anti-poaching authorities)
- Customs administrations
- Anti-corruption authorities and corruption prevention bureaus
- Offices for public prosecutors / Attorneys General
- Financial intelligence units or anti-money laundering officers
- National Police

Figure 1.1. Multi-stakeholder interviews by type

Across Singapore, Thailand, Indonesia and Viet Nam

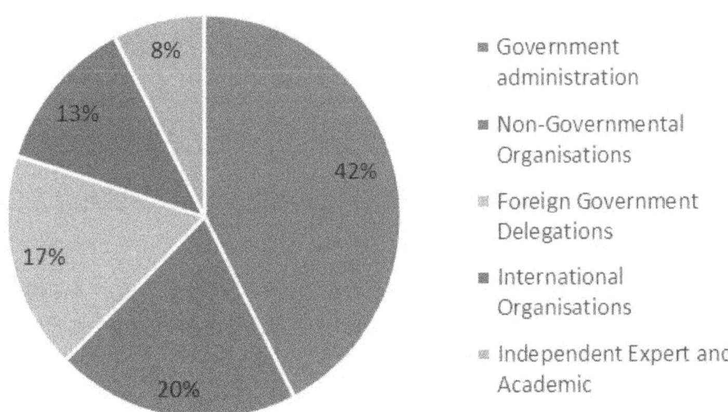

Interviews were conducted on a semi-structured basis, using a standard questionnaire to maximize the comparability of information gathered (see Annex I). The authors designed the questionnaire to target knowledge gaps identified in the desk research phase of the project including topics such as the role of corruption in the illegal wildlife trade that are not heavily covered in existing literature. Interviewees who requested not to be identified are referenced in this report through anonymised references.

The interviews gathered key insights into the everyday workings of the counter-wildlife trafficking systems and its vulnerabilities from trusted law-enforcement practitioners and conservationists active on the frontline. In analysing responses, researchers corroborated findings to cross-reference information with secondary and tertiary sources. Throughout, the analytical approach taken was both inductive and deductive. In the former case, researchers sought to draw outward from individual instances and cases of illegal wildlife trade to identify broader patterns. In the latter case, researchers looked to reason inward to the specifics from postulates about the nature of organised criminality in each location.

In some cases, the report omits specific detailed information to protect respondents and avoid compromising ongoing investigations or sources of sensitive information. However, the report draws out the broader trends and the specific implications of these responses. Where possible, footnotes linking to media and secondary sources support the information obtained from interviews.

Desk Research and Open Source Media Mapping

In addition to the semi-structured interviews, the OECD conducted preparatory desk research to inform the survey design, and to provide contextual background, statistics and historical findings on the topics of relevance in this report. The OECD used the findings from the desk research to corroborate several of the findings from the interviews throughout this report.

For the research undertaken on anti-corruption, a literature review and open media mapping was undertaken through a stocktaking of all relevant published literature, including public documents produced by international organisations, NGOs and governments. The literature review included academic papers and other relevant reports, such as briefings by domestic authorities and international declarations (i.e. reports to CITES, etc.). Twenty reports with direct relevance to anti-corruption were noted in relation to the countries or the region of study. The results of these findings are further elaborated in the chapter on the linkages between corruption and illegal wildlife trade in the region.

The report includes an open source media mapping to provide evidence of the trends on corruption in the region. The media mapping exercise was conducted with targeted word-string searches in English, French and Spanish. Searches covered the word 'ivory' AND ('poaching' OR 'seizure' OR 'trial' OR 'fraud' OR 'accused' OR 'crime' OR 'arrested' OR 'guilty' OR 'jail' OR 'suspect' OR 'bribery' OR 'laundering' OR 'corrupt'). Over 300 corruption cases were reviewed from 2008-2017, on a global scale. Of the total reported cases, 17 were specific to the four countries of focus. Six occurred in Thailand, seven in Viet Nam, and three in Indonesia.

References

FWS, U. (2019), *Illegal Wildlife Trade*, https://www.fws.gov/international/travel-and-trade/illegal-wildlife-trade.html. [14]

IPBES (2019), *Summary for policymakers of the global assessment report on biodiversity and ecosystem services of the Intergovernmental Science-Policy Platform on Biodiversity and Ecosystem Services*, https://www.ipbes.net/sites/default/files/downloads/spm_unedited_advance_for_posting_htn.pdf (accessed on 13 May 2019). [6]

Jani Actman (2016), *Poaching May Drive These 7 Species to Extinction*, https://news.nationalgeographic.com/2016/05/160520-poachers-endangered-species-extinction/ (accessed on 23 January 2019). [3]

Lin, J. (2005), *TACKLING SOUTHEAST ASIA'S ILLEGAL WILDLIFE TRADE*, http://www.cites.org/eng/disc/ (accessed on 22 January 2019). [1]

National Geographic (2018), *Poached for Its Horn, This Rare Bird Struggles to Survive*, https://www.nationalgeographic.com/magazine/2018/09/helmeted-hornbill-bird-ivory-illegal-wildlife-trade/ (accessed on 9 January 2019). [4]

OECD (2019), *Anti-corruption and integrity in the public sector*, http://www.oecd.org/corruption/ethics/. [13]

OECD (2019), *OECD Good Practices for Performance Budgeting*, OECD Publishing, Paris, https://dx.doi.org/10.1787/c90b0305-en. [12]

OECD (2019), *OECD Observatory for Public Sector Innovation: Our Work*, https://www.oecd-opsi.org/our-work/. [11]

OECD (2018), *Governance Frameworks to Counter Illicit Trade*, Illicit Trade, OECD Publishing, Paris, https://dx.doi.org/10.1787/9789264291652-en. [10]

OECD (2016), "Illicit Trade: Converging Criminal Networks", *OECD Reviews of Risk Management Policies*, http://dx.doi.org/10.1787/9789264251847-en. [9]

UN (2018), *Global indicator framework for the Sustainable Development Goals and targets of the 2030 Agenda for Sustainable Development Goals*, https://unstats.un.org/sdgs/indicators/Global%20Indicator%20Framework%20after%20refinement_Eng.pdf (accessed on 30 April 2019). [8]

UNODC (2014), *Wildlife crime worth USD 8-10 billion annually, ranking it alongside human trafficking, arms and drug dealing in terms of profits: UNODC chief*, https://www.unodc.org/unodc/en/frontpage/2014/May/wildlife-crime-worth-8-10-billion-annually.html (accessed on 13 May 2019). [7]

UNODC (2013), *Transnational organized crime: the globalized illegal economy*, https://www.unodc.org/toc/en/crimes/organized-crime.html (accessed on 4 December 2018). [2]

WWF (2019), *Rhino: Species Facts WWF*, https://www.worldwildlife.org/species/rhino (accessed on 30 April 2019). [5]

Notes

[1] Ten of eleven countries in Southeast Asia are Members of ASEAN, with the exception of Timor-Leste which is an observer Member.

[2] These include the four species of Asian Pangolin: the Chinese or Formosan Pangolin (Critically Endangered); the Malayan or Sunda Pangolin (Critically Endangered); the Indian or Thick-Tailed Pangolin (Endangered); and the Palawan or Philippine Pangolin (Endangered).

[3] Some organisations use Illegal Wildlife Trade to cover 'the gamut from illegal logging of protected forests to supply the demand for exotic woods, to the illegal fishing of endangered marine life for food, and the poaching of elephants to supply the demand for ivory' (FWS, 2019[14]). Others distinguish between terrestrial species (IWT), aquatic species (illegal fishing) and timber (illegal logging).

2 Key Findings and Detailed Recommendations

This chapter provides summary of the key findings from the chapters in this report, and offers a series of detailed recommendations for government policymakers, international organisations and non-governmental actors.

Regional context for combatting the illegal wildlife trade

Southeast Asia includes countries that are at once sources of endangered species, as well as transit points and destination markets for illegal wildlife products. This means that enforcement is a mixture of environmental protection, border control measures and market surveillance. The combined scale of the illegal wildlife trade in the region has been estimated to account for up to 25% of the global illicit market in wildlife products (Lin, 2005[1]). Illegal logging and export of exotic woods across Southeast Asia is depleting forests at an unprecedented rate due in part to a worsening poaching and snaring crisis. Illegally trapped wildlife from across the region are exported and transited, often through fraudulent certification schemes, legal loopholes and corruption among state officials. Finally, as a consumption hot-spot, wildlife products across Southeast Asia are consumed in increasing volumes and sold for growing value due to rising incomes among middle classes.

The consumption and poaching patterns across the countries studied are determined by preferences, and domestic and foreign demand factors that change over time and evolve in response to risks and incentives. For example, in Thailand, there is strong demand for ivory jewellery, whereas in Indonesia, millions of birds are traded in open markets for keeping as pets (WildAid, 2018[2]) (Rentschlar et al., 2018[3]). A sharp rise in demand from China for helmeted hornbills (i.e. the “ivory hornbill”) from Indonesia has led to the recent listing of this bird as Critically Endangered (Beastall et al., 2016[4]).

There are four main categories of consumption for illegal wildlife parts, each of which implies a role for a regulatory agency of a different industrial sector:

- Consumption for clothing and luxury items (i.e. luxury goods for display)
- Consumption for health and treatment of ailments
- Consumption for food and beverage
- Keeping of live specimens for exotic pets or zoos

Many of the same criminal syndicates that smuggle illegal wildlife from different continents abuse and destroy the biodiversity within Southeast Asian countries. For example, traders and vendors of African ivory also engage in domestic trafficking of local tiger parts, Asian birds, and Asian species of pangolin. In Viet Nam, poaching (and deforestation) has led to over 400 wild species of animals being listed as endangered and threatened. In Indonesia, poachers kill thousands of endangered and critically endangered pangolins annually and sell them in regional markets in nearby Viet Nam and China.

Across the focus countries, major transit hubs funnel illegal wildlife trade products into the region for refining, distribution and sale. Complex transit schemes are used across the region to conceal the origin of goods from authorities, including the use of registered companies to import and re-consign goods in Free Trade Zones (Sinagpore AVA, 2018[5]). Increased integration into global trade chains has outpaced developments of stronger institutional capacities in the focus countries required to enforce wildlife crimes. In countries with many islands and dense commercial maritime traffic, border control can be a practical challenge.

Management and responsibilities for enforcing laws and regulations to curb the illegal wildlife trade, and ancillary investigations, are generally structured across multiple agencies and departments. The exception is Singapore, where management of illegal wildlife trade is centrally structured and managed by the CITES management authorities. In the other countries, co-responsibility for enforcing laws against the illegal wildlife trade is pervasive, with the lead agency determined on where along the trade chain the illegal wildlife is located. Most frequently, the government agencies with responsibilities for policy, enforcement and investigations are the CITES Management Authorities and the national police administrations, but numerous institutions could potentially be involved in prevention of the illegal wildlife trade, with different remits and responsibilities for each agency or ministry.

Multi Agency Co-ordination and Multi-National Co-operation: keys to tackling the illegal wildlife trade

As is the case with investigating other forms of transnational organized crime, co-operation across law enforcement agencies is key to gather evidence across geographic and statutory jurisdictions. The involvement of multiple government agencies and other actors (such as international organisations and non-governmental organisations) has enhanced the effectiveness of investigations and prosecutions. Multi-national co-ordination among like-minded agencies such as police, CITES management authorities, and other can widen the net of suspects involved, deepen the ability to investigate and provide wider access to serious criminal charges.

In some cases, governments have formalized multi-agency task forces in response to internal and external pressures. These Wildlife Enforcement Networks (WENs)[1] generally involve relevant partner agencies such as police, customs, CITES authorities, prosecutors' offices and, in some cases, financial intelligence units and anti-corruption agencies. Of the cases studied across Indonesia, Singapore, Thailand and Viet Nam, findings suggest that successful anti-IWT efforts (measured in successful prosecutions, length of penalty and size of monetary penalties) rely on a pro-active investigation, frequent co-ordination, and multi-pronged prosecution.

Multi-national co-operation is also vital for the successful investigation and prosecution of illegal wildlife trade as a transnational organised crime. There are several avenues for multi-national co-operation, from formal Mutual Legal Assistance Treaties (MLATs), to informal networks of law enforcement officials. For formal exchanges of information in the criminal justice pathway, MLATs allow the exchange of evidence and information for the criminal justice pathway. In the informal networks of law enforcement officials, law enforcement officials exchange information and intelligence with one another for investigations and tip-offs, or joint operations. In some cases, international co-ordination has been facilitated through multi-lateral agreements, and in other instances through bi-lateral co-operation.

There are mixed results on the uptake and performance of multi-agency task forces

Despite the stated existence of multi-agency task forces or networks in several countries, the recorded use of these inter-agency structures is infrequent. Pro-active investigations are few and the vast majority of wildlife crimes are prosecuted in silos. In such cases, governments do not rely on a broader charge sheet for increasing penalties.

In some exceptional cases, there have been cases of effective multi-agency co-ordination which have led to strong results. For example, the Thailand WEN has been used in several cases for the pro-active investigation and prosecution complex illegal wildlife trade cases, which have involved national police, customs, forestry and environment or CITES officials, attorney generals' office and financial intelligence units. Consequently, sanctions have involved lengthy jail terms and asset seizures and forfeitures.

International Co-operation at a regional level (among ASEAN members) is progressing, but further efforts are needed to ensure successful co-operation against illegal wildlife trade

The ASEAN Experts Group on CITES (previously the ASEAN WEN) has facilitated the exchange of relevant information across CITES enforcement officials. However, CITES management agencies are not well equipped to handle or co-ordinate transnational criminal investigations. Therefore, further international co-ordination among police administrations is necessary. A Working Group on Illicit Trafficking in Wildlife and Timber was recently created under the leadership of Thailand within the ASEAN Senior Officials Meeting on Transnational Organised Crime (SOMTC) in 2018. The Working Group's mandate and ambitions to tackle wildlife crime from an international law enforcement angle highlights a shifting attitude towards environmental crime as a serious form of transnational crime and reflects a positive development in potential international law enforcement co-operation. However, law enforcement co-operation through ASEAN would require dedicated and structured action plans and performance monitoring (such as joint-investigations, joint operations and prosecutions) for effective deployment and action.

Bi-lateral co-operation is relatively strong at the regional level, but gaps remain between illegal wildlife trade counterparts further afield in Africa and Europe

ASEAN countries have established a number of bi-lateral information sharing arrangements among each other in both a formal and informal manner. All of the focus countries have established reciprocal MLATs. Officials in CITES authorities, customs and police use a number of information sharing approaches, from INTEPROL secure messages to WhatsApp chats to keep in touch. Closer co-operation has been facilitated through face-to-face meetings focusing on wildlife crime through fora such as APEC, ASEAN, and regional training and capacity building workshops.

Bi-lateral co-operation between the focus countries and countries outside of the ASEAN region is significantly weaker. For instance, officials reported communication gaps and fewer MLATs between ASEAN and key transit countries and source countries beyond the region. Perceptions of corruption and mistrust among counterparts adds to difficulties in information exchanges across borders[2].

Throughout all countries, there is an important role for non-government actors in the wildlife enforcement process

Working relationships between non-governmental wildlife NGOs, relevant intergovernmental organisations can lead to successful enforcement cases with fewer resources or limited government capacities. NGOs and intergovernmental organisations offer expertise, knowledge and programming to enhance institutional capacities of governments to tackle illegal wildlife trade and bridge a number of gaps in resources (which are often spread-thin for environmental crimes). In all focus countries, there are positive linkages between the engagement of non-governmental actors and outcomes for illegal wildlife trade cases. In many high-profile "Kingpin" arrests and prosecutions that were discussed in interviews, the OECD found that non-governmental actors had been involved in providing subject matter expertise, intelligence or information that is critical to the success of these cases[3].

Intergovernmental organisations have had a positive impact by supporting training activities, capacity building and strategic policy development for relevant agencies[4]. Many of these organisations offer a network of international counterparts with whom national agencies and officials can liaise. NGOs offer highly specialized operational capabilities such as intelligence gathering with high tech and low tech devices, investigative assistance, expert legal reviews of environmental laws and court case development.

Non-governmental actors, particularly those working closely with civil society help to provide added transparency and visibility for illegal wildlife trade cases in the media and among communities to raise awareness. While NGOs and Intergovernmental organisations cannot replace the institutional capacities required from relevant agencies, their positive engagement signals a well-synchronised alignment of objectives between the public sector and engaged stakeholders committed to reducing environmental crimes.

Recommendations

- Create and develop a model of inter-agency co-operation to combat the illegal wildlife trade that involves ministries and agencies mentioned in the INTERPOL NEST model.
- In all multi-agency structures, include non-traditional actors such as anti-corruption authorities and financial intelligence units.
- Strengthen the uptake of multi-agency approaches to combatting the illegal wildlife trade with strategic planning, measurable targets and timelines of illegal wildlife trade cases, investigations and prosecutions. These strategic documents should include metrics for success, including, but not limited to: the number of successful prosecutions per year; number of money laundering investigations; use of instances illegal wildlife trade charged as organized crime and; number of corruption cases.
- Establish performance budgeting: link budgets and budget approval processes to desired outcomes, in order to achieve complex objectives that may require inter-ministerial collaboration. These methods are outlined within the OECD report "Good practises for performance budgeting."
- Center of Government should promote a management culture focusing on performance and performance measurement. Incentives should be aligned to performance, and under-performance and missed-targets for investigations and prosecutions should be addressed through problem-solving rather than individual rewards of penalties .
- Develop an international framework for reporting standards in consultation with relevant experts and officials. This framework should look beyond seizure incidents and values. Performance reporting and statistics could include the number of successful prosecutions, number of corruption prosecutions and value of assets seized.
- Government authorities with responsibility for illegal wildlife trade should conduct a gap and needs analysis for legal information sharing instruments. To enhance trust and abilities to share operational information across borders with source countries, further working-level meetings are necessary to build networks of officials connecting source, transit and destination regions to facilitate closer ties and operational exchanges among law enforcement officials.
- Countries should continue to support the engagement of NGOs and IOs throughout the illegal wildlife trade enforcement process, and international community should continue to support NGOs that foster collaborative approaches to illegal wildlife trade with governments.
- The international conservation community should reinforce its focus to strengthen policies, legal frameworks and enforcement capacities to deter and combat the illegal wildlife trade in Southeast Asia. This should include a rebalancing of attention, moving towards anti-poaching, anti-corruption, anti-trafficking and anti-money-laundering programming in market countries in Southeast Asia.
- Increase dialogue between central government agencies and key decision makers to strengthen political will to tackle the illegal wildlife trade. This should involve non-traditional actors to discuss strategic approaches to wildlife crime, including criminal justice officers and judges, national development agencies, public security ministries, ministries of finance and revenue, and financial intelligence units.

Closing gaps in the legal and regulatory framework is essential to overcoming wildlife crime and preventing opportunities for criminal entrepreneurs

The focus countries are party to a number of International Legal Frameworks, including CITES, UN Convention against Corruption and the UN Convention on Transnational Organised Crime. Generally, the criminal sanctions available to punish traffickers are proportionate and deterrent. With the exception of Singapore, all focus countries treat illegal wildlife trade as a serious offense according to the UN Convection on Transnational Organized Crime (carrying maximum penalties in excess of four years' jail time). Furthermore, illegal wildlife trade can also be considered a predicate offense under Money Laundering laws in all four countries[5].

However, the deterrence of wildlife crime is significantly lessened by the inability of courts to prosecute or hand down lengthy or costly penalties. There are numerous gaps in the effectiveness of the domestic legal frameworks in all of the four countries observed. Legal loopholes can take the form of overlapping laws, ineffective legislation or opportunities for fraud and corruption in regulation and licensing schemes. These gaps and loopholes allow grey markets to flourish and create strong profit incentives for criminal entrepreneurs to brazenly operate under the guise of legitimate business dealings.

In several of the select focus countries, the enforcement of CITES Appendix Species only occurs at national borders and domestic trade is regulated by separate, less-stringent laws. Consequently, traffickers sell smuggled CITES listed wildlife products in open marketplaces because there is no way of proving their illicit origins. Consumers in open markets buy fraudulently labelled "captive bred" species which have effectively been laundered into a legal supply chain.

Under specific circumstances, there are laws for legal ivory sales in all four countries[6]. These laws have been widely abused as a loophole for traffickers to commercially sell illegal ivory into legal channels and stocks. Wildlife management authorities report that these laws are not enforceable, as they not have the capacity or the technologies to differentiate licit from illicitly sourced ivory on a commercial scale, particularly for carved ivory.

Local species fall victim to loopholes through captive breeding schemes

Criminal networks use licenses fraudulently obtained for so-called sanctuaries, zoos and research facilities to capture, breed and sell illegal wildlife products. For example, tigers and Asian black bears are "farmed" for purported use in scientific research or for educational purposes in zoos. However, due to ineffective regulatory oversight, these facilities are in fact used to exploit wildlife in a lucrative illicit market for animal parts, products, and pets.

Legal reforms to close gaps are emerging, but a number of challenges and inconsistencies remain

Governments are beginning to recognize the shortfalls of current laws. For example, Thailand has recently implemented legislation to tighten restrictions on the sale and displaying of ivory in storefronts. Since the legislation went into place, the number of vendors observed has dropped considerably. In Singapore and Viet Nam, governments are reported to be considering an outright ban on the sale of ivory. This would prohibit the open sale of any pre-CITES convention ivory that is presently legal for use.

Despite the efforts to address a number of legal loopholes, large gaps are likely to remain without significant reforms to laws, practises and policies. Many of the problematic legal frameworks in place appear to have been implemented without due consideration for the resources or the practical steps required for their enforcement and verification. Further changes are needed to remedy the status of illegal wildlife trade products being sold through legal channels across all countries of focus.

Recommendation

- In response to the open sale of endangered species in domestic markets, introduce legislative amendments that ensure that current wildlife protection laws and penalties make direct reference to all CITES category species (with relevant treatment by category) instead of the current laws which list only a limited number of wildlife species.
- In response to the failure to control legal channels of ivory products due to persistent loopholes, examine the costs and benefits of an outright ban on the sale of all ivory products regardless of origin or date of kill.
- To ensure the identification of ivory products that may have been legally acquired, deploy stringent guidelines for the registration, tracking and tracing of ivory pieces. Use vendor and consumer level fines and seizures if compliant certificates are not produced upon request.
- Introduce capacities and exchange practises on use technological solutions to identify and differentiate new ivory from older ivory, and to identify African ivory to facilitate enforcement actions.
    - In countries where there are reports of zoos and sanctuaries and captive breeding facilities used in illegal wildlife trade, develop a stricter (and enforceable) licensing guideline for the keeping of endangered species. The license application process should include stringent background checks and checklists for suspicious “red flags”
- Strengthen the traceability and monitoring for captive breeding facilities and implement a better system of oversight for breeders. Approve licenses based on scientific proof-of-concept. Expire current licenses if reasonable justifications or assurances cannot be given.
- Conduct internal integrity reviews of license granting officers recognising the heightened incentives for corruption to obtain licenses.
- Given legal loopholes in domestic markets, governments should consider the integration of significantly more CITES authority environmental enforcement officers at ports of entry in consideration of the fact that national points of entry are often the last and only line of defence against the entry and sale of illegal wildlife trade products.

Targeted efforts are needed to address corruption, which continues to facilitate the Illegal Wildlife Trade in Southeast Asia

A 2018 OECD report on illegal wildlife trade and corruption confirmed the important and central role of corruption risks in source and transit countries for illegal wildlife trade across sub-Saharan Africa. Similarly, evidence collected by the OECD in three of the four focus countries in Southeast Asia also suggests that Corruption facilitates the entry, licensing and trafficking of illegal wildlife trade in the region. Through a multi-methods approach, which included open source data collection and in-person interviews with over 90 experts in government and three anti-corruption agencies, the research suggests a number of un-mitigated corruption risks along the trade chain as illegal wildlife trade makes its way to the end-user markets.

The body of evidence for corruption in illegal wildlife trade remains small and anecdotal

There is a dearth of quantitative data on corruption in Southeast Asia. Despite a number of cited corruption risks identified by relevant experts and officials that highlighted the modus operandi of criminal syndicates and corrupt actors, the authors were able to confirm just five cases of corruption investigations for wildlife crime[7]. Research in this field is also significantly lower than for other regions. In the OECD literature review conducted for this study, the OECD found approximately 20 reports of relevance on this topic in comparison with over 100 articles for the previous 2018 OECD report on this same topic in Southern and Eastern Africa.

OECD findings point to high corruption risks at national border crossings

OECD research indicates that corruption occurs in certain hotspots at national border crossings such as airports, inland border crossings and (likely) seaports. A number of large-scale seizures have taken place at ports, airports and land border crossings where several public sector officials have been arrested for involvement in illegal wildlife trade. Officials accept bribes in exchange for allowing goods to pass through, or to accompany the goods through checkpoints to avoid scrutiny. General corruption schemes, such as bribery for "red-tape" reduction and expedited clearance at borders pose an overall risk to the entry of illicit trade as well, which includes illegal wildlife trade products among other forms of environmental crime (such as illegal logging).

Government officials in airports are at a high risk of corruption. Several schemes have been uncovered that implicate government officials, such as customs, environment officials, police) in bribery and illegal wildlife trade trafficking schemes. Private sector actors in positions of trust are involved in corruption risks. Criminal conspiracies at large airports involving baggage handlers are a known risk. At land border crossings, corruption facilitates the regional movement of illegal wildlife trade products from one Southeast Asian country into the next. Levels of corruption among customs are an important risk to the integrity of the trade chain for illegal wildlife trade products and all other forms of illicit trade.

Investigations continue to focus on the predicate offense, instead of the underlying corruption risks (and corrupt actors)

The majority of charges and prosecutions that involve public officials are for wildlife trafficking offenses instead of corruption crimes such as bribery, embezzlement or abuse of authority. Law enforcement for illegal wildlife trade remains firmly on the predicate offences, and catching the offenders "red handed", often ignoring any gross violations of public trust committed by officials.

Awareness of corruption and wildlife crime is increasing, but at a national level, more anti-corruption efforts are needed

Despite recognition at the multilateral level (e.g. CITES or G20) that illegal wildlife trade is facilitated by corruption, in nearly all of the anti-corruption agencies consulted, illegal wildlife trade does not feature as a high-level priority among many other competing issues. There is no strong political will or programming to support anti-corruption and illegal wildlife trade in Southeast Asia.

The perception of illegal wildlife trade among the anti-corruption authorities interviewed is that wildlife crimes are a lower priority in comparison with other corruption scenarios. In many cases, public corruption involving illegal wildlife trade does not meet the criteria set by administrations to trigger investigations into alleged corrupt acts.

Progress has been made in some countries. In Thailand, the National Anti-corruption Commission (NACC) enacted reforms to create a Bureau dedicated exclusively to environmental crime, which is staffed with subject-matter experts. In Indonesia, the anti-corruption commission (KPK) is a member of the "multi-door" inter-agency approach to wildlife crime. Despite advances, progress to address and prosecute corruption remains slow. Only a handful of cases in Thailand and Viet Nam have charged public officials with corruption related to wildlife crime.

Corruption remains a sensitive topic of discussion in the countries of focus nonetheless public dialogues are shifting amid broader international recognition of corruption risks. Civil society actors and international organisations have helped to enhance the visibility of wildlife crime. Increasing media attention is also contributing to a growing public recognition of the damages caused by corruption. A number of international organisations and NGOs have assisted in mobilising public opinion and support against corruption and wildlife crime; however, there are no known initiatives or capacity building schemes aimed at addressing illegal wildlife trade corruption risks head-on.

Recommendations

- Produce a national anti-corruption strategy for environmental crimes, with specific guidelines for illegal wildlife trade, describing a role for anti-corruption authorities.
- Strengthen co-operation between anti-corruption authorities and wildlife conservation actors through meetings and regular exchanges of expertise and programming. Ensure that anti-corruption authorities are members of multi-agency task forces.
    - Prioritise systematic collection of corruption incident data on an ongoing basis to quantify the number of cases relating to corruption and illegal wildlife trade in Southeast Asia.
- Encourage an active role for civil society and NGOs in drawing attention to corruption and to provide programming and expertise for investigators. Allow third-party observers and NGOs with legal expertise to monitor court cases and flag suspicious activities or outcomes during cases under investigation and before the courts.
- Integrate the prosecution and sentencing of public officials involved in illegal wildlife trade schemes as part of the broader anti-corruption campaigns underway in the countries of focus. Highlight the estimated value, ecological and economic impact of repeat offenses as reasons for referral and investigation within anti-corruption agencies.

Investigations into the illicit financial flows and money laundering investigations are necessary to deter and prosecute wildlife crime in full

Investigations into money laundering and the asset seizure or proceeds of crime are powerful tools that enhance institutional capacities against transnational organized crime and illicit trade in all goods. Wildlife crime is a predicate offense in all four countries studied[8]. However, 'follow the money' approaches to wildlife crime are rare.

Financial investigations, asset seizures and money laundering investigations remain the exception to the rule in the region

Financial Investigation Units (FIUs) feature on multi-agency task forces in two of the four countries studied. However, FIUs or financial investigations by other relevant authorities are rarely undertaken. Findings suggest that relevant officers lack the expertise, capacities, resources, and political support to conduct parallel financial investigations in response to wildlife crime on a consistent basis. Other environmental crimes such as illegal logging cases have been a key area of focus for financial investigations units in several cases across the countries studied due to the perceived costs and revenue loss estimates which are used to justify the involvement of FIUs.

Of the countries studied, Thailand is the only country that has successfully employed financial investigations and asset seizure under anti-money laundering legislation for wildlife crimes. Indonesia's FIU is also a member of the national multi-agency task force on environmental crime (the "multi-door process"); however, they have not yet been engaged in any wildlife crime cases. In Singapore and Viet Nam, respondents noted that financial investigations units are not included in wildlife enforcement networks and are not core actors in tackling illegal wildlife trade.

At the international level, knowledge of money laundering and wildlife crime is growing, however this does not translate into action on the ground

At the international level, money laundering is widely recognized as a key facilitator of wildlife crime. For example, the World Bank and other consortiums such as the International Consortium on Combatting Wildlife Crime (ICCWC) partner organizations identify money-laundering cases as one of the most effective ways of effectively prosecuting wildlife crime. Despite this recognition among the international conservation community, the Financial Action Task Force (FATF) Style Regional Body (FSRB), the Asia Pacific Group (APG) on money laundering notes that over 70% of 45 FIUs responding to a survey do not find illegal wildlife trade to be a serious money laundering threat. These findings suggest that there is a continued implementation and prioritisation gap among relevant authorities. It remains clear that financial investigations have a role to play in tackling wildlife crime but existing efforts are not sufficient.

Recent private sector initiatives highlight a willingness of the financial sector to engage against illegal wildlife trade, but more effort is needed from regional private sector actors

Financial institutions play a key role in identifying suspicious transactions and reporting risks to governments for money laundering. A recently launched private sector Wildlife Crime Financial Task Force was set up through co-ordination between a number of NGOs and financial institutions under the aegis of the United for Wildlife Project. The Task Force's objectives include raising awareness; develop training; and support policy development for illegal wildlife trade and money laundering. Of the 22 financial sector signatories, three are financial institutions based in the countries of focus of Southeast Asia.

The inclusion of the financial sector is an important component of anti-money laundering efforts to tackle the financing and proceeds of crime from wildlife crime. However, due to the fact that there are relatively few signatories from financial institutions from Asia, the effectiveness of this initiative may be limited by omission of a critical part of the global illegal wildlife trade supply chain.

Recommendations

- Treat illegal wildlife trade as a form of transnational organized crime, and conduct money laundering risk assessments for each case.
- Elevate illegal wildlife trade as an economic crime (and priority risk for FIUs). Develop methods to calculate the economic and financial impact of illegal wildlife trade by looking at such factors as long-term economic consequences for bio-diversity, tourism revenue, and losses from corruption.
- Include FIUs as part of multi-agency task forces. Strategic action plans for illegal wildlife trade should set targets that also include money-laundering investigations or asset identification or seizure as a performance objective to tackling illegal wildlife trade.
    - International coalitions should conduct 'synthetic' money laundering risk reviews highlighting likely proceeds of crime involved, and potential typologies for suspicious transaction types and share these reports with FIUs in the region.
- Countries should leverage the expertise and global networks of the Asia Pacific Group (APG), a FATF Style Regional Body (FSRB) to build guidance on implementation of the FATF Recommendations in the context of the illegal wildlife trade illegal wildlife trade. Members could discuss an in-depth study on risks, trends and methods of environmental crimes and money laundering, for use by FIUs and competent authorities.
- Work closely with banks and other financial institutions, as well as NGOs to strengthen practises in money laundering investigations for wildlife crime.

- Countries should incentivise the engagement of regionally based Southeast Asia-based financial institutions, as well as financial intermediaries (such as clearing-houses) in the Financial Task Force, and work with private sector bodies to increase awareness, identify risks, strengthen capacities and share typologies.

References

ASEAN-WEN, Freeland (2016), *ASEAN Handbook on Legal Cooperation to Combat Illegal Wildlife Trade*. [6]

Beastall, C. et al. (2016), "Trade in the Helmeted Hornbill Rhinoplax vigil : the 'ivory hornbill'", *Bird Conservation International*, Vol. 26, pp. 137-146, http://dx.doi.org/10.1017/S0959270916000010. [4]

Lin, J. (2005), *Tackling Southeast Asia's illegal wildlife trade*, http://www.aseansec. [1]

Rentschlar, K. et al. (2018), "A Silent Morning: The Songbird Trade in Kalimantan, Indonesia", *Tropical Conservation Science*, Vol. 11, p. 194008291775390, http://dx.doi.org/10.1177/1940082917753909. [3]

Sinagpore AVA (2018), *Interview with Singapore Agriculture and Veterinary Authority, Singapore, October 15, 2018*. [5]

WildAid (2018), *Ivory Demand In Thailand*, https://wildaid.org/wp-content/uploads/2017/09/Thailand-Survey-EN.pdf (accessed on 22 November 2018). [2]

Notes

[1] Also known as "multi-door approaches", also known as inter-agency forces.

[2] Officials have pointed to examples where evidence and information for prosecutions is vulnerable to corruption risks in several source countries. In one case, authorities interdicted an IWT shipment containing previously seized products stolen from courtroom stocks and smuggled back into Southeast Asia.

[3] Indeed, non-government actors are well-positioned to assist with IWT cases due to the fact that that governments must compete with many different priorities whereas these specialized groups (many of which are composed of former law enforcement and environment officials) focus on conducting intelligence gathering and network analysis in a highly specific field of expertise.

[4] The studies conducted in all the focus countries found that non-governmental bodies, in particular wildlife NGOs play a critical role in first co-ordinating among relevant bodies, secondly in providing subject matter expertise and intelligence, and third providing support for court cases that can be used for the successful prosecution of wildlife crimes.

[5] Either directly or by inference (ASEAN-WEN, Freeland, 2016[6]).

[6] Depending on the country, these stocks could be from pre-CITES convention "vintage" ivory stocks, or from local "beasts of burden" domesticated Asian elephants whose ivory can be commercially sold.

[7] Cases here public officials have been arrested and charged in connection to acts of corruption, or where an official investigation has been opened.

[8] Can include inferred definition of predicate offense

3 Multi-Agency and International Co-operation

This chapter explores the concept of co-operation and co-ordination among relevant institutional actors both within a country and in the international setting. Firstly, it examines multi-agency co-operation among relevant domestic agencies, secondly, it studies co-operation among relevant international stakeholders as a response to the transnational organized crimes related to the illegal wildlife trade. Throughout, this chapter also considers the role of non-governmental actors, including international organisations and non-governmental organisations, and their impact in countering illegal wildlife trade.

Introduction

There are a number of benefits to multi-agency and international co-operation to tackle illegal wildlife trade. At a domestic level, the early and close interaction of relevant competent authorities such as wildlife enforcement agencies, police, customs, financial intelligence units, anti-corruption agencies and public prosecutors can facilitate complex and multi-pronged investigations against organized criminal actors. As noted in a previous OECD report on illegal wildlife trade, the use of multi-agency task forces also increases the integrity of investigations by preventing corruption risks due to separate reporting hierarchies in the different agencies involved (OECD, 2018[1]). Multi-agency co-operation is also valuable across borders: international law enforcement networks, intelligence exchange, co-ordinated investigations, transfer of evidence through legal assistance treaties and controlled deliveries are several practical illustrations of the how international co-operation can improve institutional capacities to address illegal wildlife trade (UNODC, 2015[2]). In addition to government-to-government co-ordination, authorities also stand to benefit from co-ordination with relevant NGOs and intergovernmental organisations. As this chapter highlights, intergovernmental actors such as INTERPOL, UN Office of Drugs and Crime (UNODC), UN Development Programme (UNDP) and others can provide expertise and training, capacity building and secure international information exchange platforms for law enforcement officials. NGOs can offer field expertise, research, training, and connect a broader range of contacts that is necessary to identify key actors in complex schemes and to carry-out investigations in specific conservation areas.

This chapter first examines how each of the Southeast Asian countries leverages multi-agency co-ordination, and provides a reflection on the functioning of each model of inter-agency co-operation in each country. Secondly, the chapter reviews the forms of regional and international co-ordination efforts against illegal wildlife trade. The sections below provide analysis of multi-agency co-operation and co-ordination among relevant national agencies within each focus country.

Multi-Agency Co-ordination and Task Forces

With the exception of Singapore, the countries studied have formalized multi-agency task forces into "wildlife enforcement networks" (WENs) to coordinate law enforcement efforts against illegal wildlife trade under different names. These WENs are implemented to co-ordinate law enforcement efforts and investigations against wildlife crimes, and are designed to integrate a number of relevant agencies.

The structure and composition of WENs are guided by roadmaps and high-level policy guidance from a range of international organisations. For example, the 2015 UN General Assembly Resolution on Tackling Illegal Wildlife Trade "*encourages Member States (…) to establish national level inter-agency wildlife crime task forces, consistent with national legislation*" (UN, 2015[3]). Policy instruments such as the EU Action Plan against Wildlife Trafficking, also call for "*a coordination mechanism (such as an inter-agency task force and/or Memorandum of Understanding) between the relevant agencies (customs, inspection services, police, CITES management and enforcement authorities)"* (EU, 2016[4]).

Practical guides for the creation and implementation of inter-agency task forces is outlined by INTERPOL, whose National Environmental Security Task Force (NEST) model is outlined below:

Box 3.1. INTERPOL National Environmental Security Seminars (NESS) and National Environmental Task Force (NEST)

INTERPOL has co-ordinated several National Environmental Security Seminars (NESS) bringing together police, customs, environmental agencies, prosecutors, non-governmental organizations and intergovernmental partners to enhance cooperation and communication among national agencies focusing on environmental crime. These seminars encourage the creation of a National Environmental Security Task Forces (NEST) within member countries with multi-agency contact points for joint investigations and enhanced national cooperation (INTERPOL, 2013[5]). NEST Task Forces recommend the inclusion of the following agencies and administrations into the task force:

- Police
- Customs
- Environment Agencies
- Prosecutor
- Other specialized agencies

Inter-agency co-ordination through the INTERPOL NEST model lodges wildlife crime within a broader environmental crime agenda, speaking to crime convergence zones, and recognizes the linkages with other governance issues and forms of illicit trade. For example, forest clearance and illegal logging is closely associated with the illegal killing of wildlife, which may be addressed by converging relevant institutions into a common forum to elevate the prioritisation of wildlife crimes. The INTERPOL NEST structures are reflected in the multi-agency task forces in several countries across Southeast Asia (such as Viet Nam, Thailand and Indonesia). As noted in the sections below, several of these inter-agency task forces (called WENs, or Multi-door approaches) include anti-corruption agencies as well as Financial Intelligence Units. These are not explicitly called for in the NEST model, however their inclusion in inter-agency task forces is clearly beneficial to improving institutional co-operation among relevant administrations to tackle wildlife crime, and could stand out as a best practise in other models.

The below section evaluates the use of WENs in each country, and the use of a non-WEN system in Singapore.

Thailand

The enforcement of illegal wildlife trade in Thailand is co-ordinated on a formal basis through the Thailand Wildlife Enforcement Network (Thailand WEN). The WEN leverages the expertise of several agencies for illegal wildlife trade enforcement, upstream and downstream investigations and prosecutions. The WEN enjoys a relatively high-level of communication and co-ordination between member agencies. The relevant competent authorities designated in the Thai WEN model are:

- Department of National Parks, Wildlife and Plant Conservation (and relevant sub-bodies)
- Department of Fisheries
- Royal Thai Customs
- Royal Thai Police
- Anti-Money Laundering Authority

The Thailand WEN also has a formalized strategic operational framework in place. The WEN conducts reporting on an annual basis to the Thailand CITES authority (Department of National parks) as well as to the ASEAN CITES Working Group. The WEN holds scheduled meetings, and sets forth action plans (only available in Thai). The Thailand WEN also publishes the results of seizures, arrests, and prosecutions on a public website. This website includes the addresses for relevant contact points in the various agencies involved in countering illegal wildlife trade. It is noteworthy that the National Anti-Corruption Commission (NACC) is not a part of the Thai WEN or the National Ivory Acton Plan (NIAP). For criminal investigations and prosecutions, the Thai Royal Police's National Police Natural Resources and Environmental Crime Suppression Division (NED) is the principle actor in investigating and prosecuting wildlife crime once it has been identified.

Because of the strong interagency co-ordination established in Thailand, the agencies have reported recent successes related to illegal wildlife trade crimes, which included successful international investigations with counterparts in source countries, as well as tracing and seizure of assets and properties implicated in the crimes (Thailand AMLO, 2018[6]). The Thailand WEN investigation cited below showcases how multi-agency co-ordination through WENs has been used dismantle complex networks of transnational criminals through multi-agency co-ordination:

Box 3.2. Thailand Wildlife Enforcement Network In Action

In 2017, Thai Customs arrested a corrupt Thai Quarantine Official trying to smuggle rhino horns into the country using store-rooms and special access at the Bangkok Suvarnabhumi airport. The subsequent upstream investigation was conducted by several agencies. Through the Thailand WEN official structure, the national police's Natural Resources Environmental Crime Suppression Division worked with the customs authorities (who made the rhino seizure), the AMLO and the CITES authority (Freeland, 2018[7]) (TRAFFIC, 2018[8]). This WEN co-ordinated investigation led to the unravelling of a complex criminal network reaching back to the source country and involving a series of arrests linked to family members of a known Thai "Kingpin" in charge of one of the largest illegal wildlife trade smuggling rings in the country. The upstream investigation also linked the arrested suspects to another three corrupt officials charged with facilitating the entry of illegal wildlife trade products into the Suvarnabhumi airport (noted in an earlier example in this report).

This "Kingpin" case is one of the first and few examples of the successful use of proceeds of crime legislation in a wildlife enforcement case as well (Thailand AMLO, 2018[6]).

The involvement of wildlife and conservation NGOs in Thailand have bolstered the success of several wildlife investigations in Thailand. Non-profit organisation have provided information, intelligence and resources to a number of cases. One such organisation is the NGO Freeland Thailand, a global non-profit working on environmental crimes and human trafficking investigation. Freeland have provided information, intelligence and resources that have contributed to a number of successful anti-trafficking cases (Freeland, 2018[7]). A range of other active NGOs have also been known to bolster environmental crime investigations, either through officer training programs, investigative assistance, or intelligence and information gathering on certain known criminal groups. In Thailand, NGOs are active in the collection of tip-offs, practical "street-level" intelligence and identification of international networks. NGOs also provide expert knowledge and guidance on complex wildlife related matters before the courts.

Despite recent successes in institutional co-ordination and the engagement of NGOs such as Freeland and others, just ten high-level cases over the past eight years have involved the use of the WEN structure. According to one respondent, securing evidence and follow-up investigations are often not enough to deter illegal wildlife trade, as there are not enough investigations underway to counter illegal wildlife trade which occurs on such a large scale (TRAFFIC, 2018[8]). Respondents also noted that multi-agency co-ordination in the Thailand WEN comes at a high-cost in resources and expertise, and various agencies such as the Financial Intelligence Unit have limited resources and expertise to dedicate to a range of crimes, several of which are given greater priority from central government (Thailand AMLO, 2018[6]). Prosecution such as confiscation of proceeds of crime and asset seizure has only been successfully used in one known case (Freeland, 2018[7]).

Thailand persists as the top markets for ivory, and several open markets continue to operate for the open sale of illegally obtained wildlife products (WildAid, 2018[9]). Nevertheless, the successful investigations and prosecutions carried out by the Thailand WEN offer a regional best practise and a precedent for future investigations. The multi-agency co-ordination enjoyed through these investigations is a model that could be streamlined and built-upon reduce future costs and increase prosecutorial effectiveness. Despite this, obstacles remain from a resource allocation and prioritisation perspective, thus pointing to a greater need for sustained high-level political support for WEN-style investigations and prosecutions of wildlife crime.

Indonesia

The Indonesian "multi-door approach" is a multi-agency co-ordination framework in place for the investigation of certain environmental crimes that include illegal wildlife trade, illegal logging and forestry crimes. This framework for multi-agency co-ordination has high potential to improve the way that the government can enforce laws related to environmental protection. The multi-door strategy covers forestry, plantation, mining, spatial planning, environment, taxation, corruption and money laundering legislation (Indonesia Customs, 2018[10]) (Indonesia MEF, 2018[11]) (Indonesia PPATK, 2018[12]). The recently developed multi-door approach calls for stronger inter-agency co-ordination between the civil investigators in the Ministry of Environment (MEF). Indonesia's multi-door approach proposes a model of co-ordination and co-operation that responds to environmental crime with a broader range of offenses. The multi-door approach is composed of the following agencies:

- Indonesia National Police (INP)
- Office of the Attorney General
- Indonesia Customs
- Forestry (Indonesia MEF)
- Financial Transaction Reports and Analysis Centre (PPATK)
- Quarantine Authority
- Indonesia Anti-Corruption Commission (KPK)

The Indonesia MEF reports that eight illegal wildlife trade cases have taken place in 2018. So far no illegal wildlife trade cases have leveraged inter-agency co-ordination through the multi-door approach. As a result, the predicate offense of the illegal trade in protected plant and animal species is exclusively used (Act No. 5 /1990 on the 'Conservation of Living Resources and their Ecosystem'). Evidence suggests that penalties remain inadequate to deter complex illegal wildlife trade networks: monetary fines amount to a total of just USD $7,800 and the maximum imprisonment term for wildlife trafficking specifically against protected species is 5 years. Interviewees also note that over half of these cases have resulted in convictions with sentences of under two years (Indonesia National Police, 2018[13]) (Indonesia MEF, 2018[11]). Furthermore, as noted in the chapter on legal gaps and loopholes, the Act 5/1990 only considers the illegal trade in native species. Due to this legal loophole, any trade in non-native endangered species would not incur any criminal penalties under this legislation[1] (ASEAN-WEN, Freeland, 2016[14]).

In Indonesia, multi-agency co-ordination for wildlife crimes does take place, however it is not structured in the multi-door process. Co-ordination among relevant agencies remains *ad-hoc*[2], and reliant on existing bi-lateral ties between officials and actors in the various ministries and NGOs (Indonesia MEF, 2018[11]). Evidence suggests that the relevant Indonesian authorities such as Indonesia National Police and the MEF have a strong working relationship. Several relevant authorities also have a strong working relationship with intergovernmental organisations and non-governmental organisations that are active in environmental conservation. For example, the United Nations Development Program (UNDP) provides capacity building, policy and strategic plan development in support of improving enforcement and prosecution of wildlife and forestry crime (UNDP, 2018[15]). NGOs are also active in providing support to Indonesian authorities. For example, the NGO Wildlife Conservation Society (WCS) delivers expertise and investigative support to relevant authorities through intelligence gathering and sharing of expertise (see example below) (WCS Indonesia, 2018[16]) (Indonesia MEF, 2018[11]).

Co-ordination among NGOs and governments has led to successful, concrete law enforcement results in combatting illegal wildlife trade (Indonesia AGO, 2018[17]) (Indonesia MEF, 2018[11]). Since 2003, over 540 prosecutions of domestic poaching or trafficking and illegal wildlife trade are known to have benefitted from information and expertise provided by NGOs like WCS Indonesia and the specialized WCS Wildlife Crimes Unit (WCS Indonesia, 2017[18]). In addition certain private sector actors provide support to illegal wildlife trade investigations in Indonesia. IBM, has supplied police with new investigative technologies for a new digital "cyber patrol", such as specialized network analysis tool called the "i2" system, which is used for gathering evidence and intelligence from seized phones (Indonesia MEF, 2018[11]) (Indonesia National Police, 2018[13]) (UNDP, 2018[15]). Once seized, investigators can use the information from communications equipment to track down wider networks of actors to broaden the net of investigations and tackle illegal wildlife trade as a form of organized crime, instead of simply focusing on the single instance of wildlife crime for which the original arrest took place.

Box 3.3. Co-ordination between Indonesia Government and the WCS

The Wildlife Conservation Society's (WCS) Indonesia Wildlife Crimes Unit (WCU) works to coordinate with the national police, district police, quarantine authorities, the MEF, the financial oversight authorities and other law enforcement agencies and conservation administrations to facilitate the gathering of intelligence and information from a local informant network across several hotspots in Indonesia. The WCU also provides assistance and expertise for illegal wildlife trade related matters, and raises awareness and education of illegal wildlife trade related issues in Indonesia, particularly for domestic illegal wildlife trade trafficked out of Indonesia and into nearby destination markets. To address transnational criminal networks, the WCU also liaises directly with a close network of relevant contacts overseas to exchange information and intelligence on international trafficking cases. The WCU works with law enforcement (including district or provincial authorities) to provide intelligence in a rapid and less formal manner, as respondents have noted that official channels of information exchange can often be slow and ineffective (WCS Indonesia, 2018[16]) (Indonesia National Police, 2018[13]).

Cases

WCU has been involved in a large number of arrests and seizures to provide expert advice and guidance on the categorisation of species and the legal frameworks available for penalties and prosecutions. In 2017, WCU supported the Aviation Security in Jakarta for the arrest of a known Japanese reptile smuggler attempting to export four suitcases and a box containing 253 reptiles that included three protected species (tree pythons, tree skinks (lizard) and a pig-nosed turtle). Involvement of WCS in the process helped to deliver a two year and 11 month prison sentence and a fine of over USD $4,000.

In 2018, the WCSU WCU assisted police in the investigation and arrest of a pangolin trafficker in West Java, seizing pangolin scales and live pangolins (1.6 kg of scales and three live animals). The arrest was co-ordinated during a transaction and ended with the arrest of the trafficker (prosecution/conviction pending). WCU provided relevant information and intelligence to facilitate the arrest after several months of investigation co-ordinated with District Police (WCS WCU, 2019[19]).

Media Monitoring and Advocacy

One valuable role of the WCU has been providing journalists and media with information on illegal wildlife trade cases and prosecution results. The dissemination of this information into the media helps to make the public more aware of recent successes and prosecutions of poachers and criminal networks, and provides greater visibility to the government agencies and ministries conducting raids, seizures and arrests to counter illegal wildlife trade.

Network Analyses

The WCU team works closely with government and assists in gathering field intelligence, but also conducts cyber-monitoring using IBM i2 software systems to identify networks and to target specific individuals along the illegal wildlife trade chain.

According to intelligence and information gathered by WCS, there are two main forms of organized crime groups operating in illegal wildlife trade in Indonesia. The first group of traffickers are those who are involved in mid-level transactions and who function within the community, and are relatively poorer. These traffickers, who hunt domestic animals such as pangolins, endangered birds and reptiles often work in teams of 4-5 and they are connected via groups. They help each other out and split their earnings. Often functioning on a closed network basis. The second group are high-level, high-value traffickers of Chinese or Chinese Indonesian origin, and function along family ties with strong competition among each other. They are reported to enjoy strong protection from corrupt networks of officials, and are very wealthy. WCS notes for example that the international trade in pangolins is controlled by several Chinese Families and Vietnamese families who both export these to their respective countries (WCS Indonesia, 2018[16]).

Since it began operations in 2003, the Unit has worked with law enforcement authorities to support over 500 sting operations to arrest more than 600 wildlife trafficking criminals, with a sentencing rate of higher than 90% (WCS Indonesia, 2018[16]).

Among other forms of environmental crime, (and in contrast to the multi-door approach that has not yet been used for illegal wildlife trade) the National Task Force on Logging (created by presidential decree) has been used for several high-level multi-agency investigations. These investigations have included charges related to environmental crime, money laundering and corruption (WCS Indonesia, 2018[16]). However, in contrast to logging, illegal wildlife trade is not recognized as a similarly serious offense. Respondents from KPK noted that most illegal wildlife trade cases do not meet the minimum threshold for anti-corruption investigations. As noted earlier in this report, the KPK has a strict set of rules that at least two out of the following three conditions must be met to qualify for a Commission investigation and prosecutions (Indonesia KPK, 2018[20]). The crime in question must:

- Involve graft in excess of $US 63,000
- Involve a high level official
- Involve a crime of serious public concern

If KPK thresholds are not met, any corruption cases or allegations are handed down to Indonesia National Police or other police administrations. OECD interviews indicated however that no corruption investigations relating to illegal wildlife trade have been investigated or prosecuted at the lower level, and that capacities at the police level are severely lacking to conduct such investigations.

The multi-door model has been developed as a policy framework for co-ordination and there are no directives or requirements to deliver on targets, actions and objectives (UNDP, 2018[15]). Respondents pointed out that any successful deployment of a multi-door model would also require a strategic action plan. Such an action plan could contain a number of provisions, such as those outlined in the following framework:

Box 3.4. Example of a Strategic Action Plan Structure

As witnessed in Thailand WEN's case, the development of strategic action plans, common reporting standards and objectives is an important tool for ensuring the implementation of multi-agency task forces. Indonesia's numerous relevant authorities could consider a strategic action plan for implementing multi-agency co-ordination which could be based on a guideline for development such as the one outlined below:

Strategic Action Plan Structure

Vision: What is the stated common vision of the members of the multi-door approach?

Mission: Provide clear and achievable mission roles for each of the agencies involved, outline their position in the multi-agency structure

Objectives: Determine what actions and deliverables must take place for the multi-door approach to be considered successful Establish what action or change will occur as a result of the implementation of the plan (i.e. reduction in wildlife crime, seizure of assets, arrest of corrupt actors). Set a clear number of performance metrics (i.e. cases, numbers of prosecutions, number of agencies involved and resulting conviction rates) that move in the direction of meeting specific objectives

Strategies: What forums or meetings, task forces and communication plans are necessary to co-ordinate agencies and deliver on the set objectives

Communication of results and accountability: Establish a framework for accountability and transparency of the strategic action plan to hold agencies to account for their performance.

Singapore

Singapore's Agricultural and Veterinary Authority (AVA) is the principle agency in charge of all aspects related to enforcement of wildlife crime. The AVA enforces the Endangered Species (Import and Export) (Act Chapter 92A, 2006, revised in 2008 (ESA)[3], which lists the species and acts relevant to the illegal wildlife trade and the possession of endangered species. Singapore's approach to interagency cooperation in enforcement actions against illegal wildlife trade is distinct from the other countries surveyed in this report: there are no environmental crime task forces or wildlife enforcement networks in place. Instead, the AVA provides instruction, training and expertise to other relevant authorities such as the Immigration and Customs Authority (ICA) and the national police for targeted interceptions. Singapore is therefore the only country of this study that does not have a multi-agency structure to tackle illegal wildlife trade.

On measures related to enforcement Singapore engages with several other agencies. In cases where illegal wildlife trade is suspected at the various shipping ports or land border crossings or at Changi International Airport, the AVA co-ordinates with ICA to conduct seizures or arrests at national points of entry. Within the national territory, the AVA conducts enforcement in co-ordination with the National Police to accompany the Agency make arrests and raids. The AVA does not have authority to pursue suspects and can only conduct arrests or detentions in specific un-contentious scenarios[4].

There have been no known cases of illegal wildlife trade convictions in Singapore that have involved charges of organized criminal activity, money laundering offenses or offenses other than those set forth in the Revised 2008 ESA. Singapore AVA does not have a number of the capacities required to conduct transnational criminal investigations into wildlife crimes, or to independently arrest persons on suspicion of wildlife trafficking. There are no inter-agency structures of co-ordination that mandate agencies such as National Police or Customs to work pro-actively with the AVA throughout the intelligence gathering and investigatory process, and no frameworks or objectives have been set for targeting transnational organized crime and proceeds of crime.

Despite the absence of multi-agency structures to address illegal wildlife trade from as a transnational organized crime, Singapore remains an important hub for global illegal wildlife trade flows in transit or as a destination:

Box 3.5. Large-scale illegal wildlife trade seizures in Singapore's Major Port in-route to Viet Nam

Due to its central role in the regional economy, Singapore has been used as a hub for illegal wildlife trade as an entry point into the regional trade chain. Illegal wildlife trade products and large-scale shipments are often imported for re-export into nearby countries (ACRES, 2019[21]). Traffickers involved in this trade are often members of complex organized criminal schemes (ACRES, 2018[22]) (FD-7, 2018[23]). The original point of departure can be masked by moving through Singapore's Free Trade Zone where companies can take advantage of Singapore's strong security reputation and re-consign goods for re-export (Sinagpore AVA, 2018[24]). One expert noted that "IWT is just not on the agenda" for Singaporean national law enforcement authorities" (NG-03, 2018[25]).

Ivory Seizures in Singapore's FTZ

In 2018, in co-ordination with the ASEAN Wildlife Enforcement Network and with direction from the AVA, Singapore Customs at the Port of Singapore intercepted a large shipment of ivory in a container full of peanuts from Nigeria. Authorities seized 1,787 ivory pieces in total weighing 3.5 tons and worth over USD $2 million. The case relied on an import for re-export scheme where a Singapore-based freight forwarding company registered to a Vietnamese national would briefly import goods into Singapore's Free Trade Zone so that they could be re-consigned and masked of their origin to be subsequently exported onwards to the final destination in Viet Nam (Sinagpore AVA, 2018[24]). In the case, authorities shared information on this seizure with the Viet Nam counterparts for further investigation in the intended country of destination. No arrests or prosecutions were made as a result of this case in Singapore.

Cases involving illegal rosewood

In 2017, Singapore Customs intercepted two large-scale shipments of rosewood and other timber in-route to Viet Nam. In these two cases, over 60 species of rosewood were seized, weighing over 3,200 and 1,200 tonnes and each worth in excess of $USD 30 million (Sinagpore AVA, 2018[24]). In one case, a Singapore based company was used as a consignee, but no arrests were made as no person could be located in connection with this company in Singapore. Authorities noted that only forestry legislation (ESA) would be used in the event of a prosecution. Here, penalties would also not exceed USD 360,000 and jail term of equivalent to several months in prison would be handed down if any suspects were apprehended.

In an effort to enhance capacities and impact, the AVA co-ordinates closely and regularly with conservation NGOs that are established in the country. In particular, the Singaporean authorities work closely with the NGO 'Animal Concerns Research and Education Society' (ACRES), which provides subject matter expertise on zoological matters, analysis and case referrals to the AVA for domestic seizures. The example below highlights the important synergies between the work of wildlife authorities and local NGOs. NGOs can help to bolster the institutional capacities of relevant agencies, provide subject matter expertise, policy guidance and even support functions (such as the 24-hour illegal wildlife trade reporting hotline).

Box 3.6. ACRES NGO Co-operation with Singapore's AVA

ACRES is a domestically operating NGO that works from the community level to focus on illegal wildlife trade within Singapore. In 2017, the ACRES group identified 111 cases of live animals for sale and 483 cases of animal parts. Most of these goods are mostly advertised online, and range in price from 60$ to nearly $2,000. The NGO also works closely with various internet marketplaces and social media platforms to identify and take down advertisements for illegal wildlife trade products. On the educational side, the ACRES foundation also works through numerous channels, including through schools to raise awareness of illegal wildlife products.

On enforcement, the NGO has provided additional resourcing to illegal wildlife trade and has acted as a supporting agency to the AVA by providing relevant information and intelligence to the Singapore's wildlife enforcement agency to increase the number of cases, seizures and arrests. On the policy side, the NGO provides research and policy proposals to the AVA and through other channels in the Singaporean government. The ACRES group also staffs a 24-hour hotline to receive tip-offs from local Singaporeans on cases relating to illegal wildlife trade and other animal cruelty cases.

Viet Nam

In 2014, a directive from the Prime Minister ordered that all line ministries co-ordinate and make illegal wildlife trade a first-level priority. This co-ordination is formalized through the Viet Nam Wildlife Enforcement Network (Viet Nam WEN) chaired by the Ministry of Agriculture and Rural Development (MARD), which is the CITES management authority of Viet Nam. Recent amendments to the penal code in 2018 have also increased the penalties for illegal wildlife trade related offenses and strengthened the position of agencies to prosecute illegal wildlife trade[5]. However, in such cases, the complex organized crimes require greater institutional and investigative capacities that are predicated upon strengthened inter-agency co-ordination, exchange of information and intelligence sharing between relevant stakeholders. To this end, the CITES authority, MARD is in charge of co-ordinating and implementing anti-IWT policies and efforts for domestic and transnational organized crimes related to trafficking in wildlife products. The MARD liaises with other relevant agencies, including the Ministry of Public Safety Environmental Police, the Viet Nam Customs, Ministry of Justice and the Supreme Peoples' Procuracy.

Respondents indicated however that the Viet Nam WEN structure is not used to its fullest potential. Despite the formalized structure and the creation of the WEN, interviewees offered no instance where the WEN network was involved in law enforcement co-ordination, investigations or prosecution for offenses such as organized crime, corruption or money laundering. Officials from the MARD noted, "While the Wildlife Enforcement Network is in place to prevent wildlife crime, the investigation remains up to each organisation to undertake." (Viet Nam MARD, 2018[26]). Other experts explained that WEN member agencies "continue to operate in silos" with insufficient exchange of intelligence or relevant investigative information (IO-1, 2018[27]). As a result, in its present state, the WEN does not yet have a strategic implementation plan or operational group. These findings corroborate previous studies and reviews that find the WEN has not served its full purpose, despite the structures and networks that are enshrined in the Viet Nam WEN (World Bank, 2016[28]).

Engagement with Relevant NGOs and International Organisations (IOs)

Effective lines of communication are found between several leading wildlife NGOs and relevant authorities. For example, the NGO Education for Nature Viet Nam (ENV) as well as WCS both have important embedded roles in assisting with investigations of wildlife crimes (see box below). This co-ordination between relevant bodies and NGOs runs counter to the prevailing "silos" across enforcement agencies in Viet Nam.

Box 3.7. NGO Co-ordination in Viet Nam

Education for Nature Viet Nam (ENV)

The Viet Nam-based NGO ENV collects data on illegal wildlife trade and collects courtroom results to monitor and improve prosecution rates for illegal wildlife trade offenses. To-date, the illegal wildlife trade database contains over 13,000 data points since its creation in 2005. Since 2008, the ENV group has also operated a hot line to report illegal wildlife trade crimes. By relying on strong informal networks (both domestically and internationally), the NGO helps to provide intelligence and information to governments by offering subject matter expertise and capacities. The ENV approach is one that is based on developing non-antagonistic, constructive approaches with the government. ENV works to publicize a lot of the progress, and acts as a liaison to communicate successful cases to media in a way that ensures more accountability that positively reinforces their work without denigrating the efforts of government.

Wildlife Conservation Society Viet Nam

In Viet Nam, WCS focuses on helping to raise awareness of the costs and impacts of illegal wildlife trade while also assisting law enforcement with technical assistance, training and investigatory capacities. WCS works also at the community level, working with local leaders and co-ordinating with local environmental police working directly in the field to enhance capacities and strengthen enforcement powers, even going so far as to providing equipment to forestry officials to counter domestic illegal wildlife trade risks. WCS is particularly active in several border regions that are particularly vulnerable to illegal wildlife trade. WCS conducts information and intelligence gathering, liaising with local contacts in order to produce briefings and reports for law enforcement officials on the transnational criminal networks active in the regions. The WCS program also works closely to exchange information with its WCS China counterparts in order to tackle the serious transnational criminal elements of the trafficking networks.

International Law Enforcement Co-operation

Comprehensive international co-operation is essential to address the illegal wildlife trade. The United Nations Convention against Transnational Organized Crime (UNTOC) is the guiding treaty for addressing serious transnational organized crime in a co-ordinated manner. State parties to the UNTOC are committed to establish a comprehensive framework, which includes several elements related to international co-operation, namely extradition (Article 16), mutual legal assistance (Article 18), joint investigations (Article 19), and strengthened international co-operation among law enforcement (Article 27) (UN, 2004[29]). This section studies these various forms of international co-operation in the focus countries.

These forms of co-operation are both formal and informal. Formal co-operation takes place through official legal channels, often across judicial authorities or designated administrations thanks to international treaties. Informal co-ordination can be meetings between law enforcement officials and exchanges of practises and operational information for investigations. Both formal and informal forms of co-ordination are necessary to strengthen international co-operation against illegal wildlife trade (UNODC, 2015[2]).

Extradition and Mutual Legal Assistance

Mutual legal assistance and extradition agreements are two examples of formal international co-operation. MLATs "allow generally for the exchange of evidence and information in criminal and related matters" (US DoS, 2012[30]) For illegal wildlife trade, MLATs are the legal basis up on which countries may exchange information such as evidence, bank records, communications details and other information for use in investigations or judicial proceedings for wildlife trafficking cases. Extradition treaties set the circumstances and legal ground rules for one country surrendering an individual to another country to face prosecution for crimes committed in that country (CFR, 2019[31]). Extradition agreements can be useful for prosecuting illegal wildlife trade cases that involve members of transnational criminal syndicates operating in an international context who may be located in another country.

In 2004, all ASEAN member states enacted the Treaty on Mutual Legal Assistance in Criminality Matters by Like-Minded Member Countries. This multilateral MLAT sets the framework at a regional level for reciprocal exchanges of information for the purposes of law enforcement investigations. With the exception of Cambodia (which restricts MLATs use exclusively to drug related offenses), all ASEAN members have passed laws that enable these instruments to be used for the exchange of sensitive information to be used in court (ASEAN-WEN, Freeland, 2016[14]).

According to the Freeland and the ASEAN-WEN secretariat, a number of ASEAN countries have extradition arrangements in place. As the matrix table below shows Thailand, Viet Nam and Indonesia have arrangements with four or more countries, whereas Singapore has established an extradition arrangement with just one other country.

Table 3.1. ASEAN Bi-lateral Extradition Arrangements

	Brunei	Cambodia	Indonesia	Laos	Malaysia	Myanmar	Philippines	Singapore	Thailand	Viet Nam
Brunei					X			X		
Cambodia				X					X	X
Indonesia					X		X		X	X
Laos		X							X	X
Malaysia	X		X						X	
Myanmar										
Philippines			X						X	
Singapore	X									
Thailand		X	X	X	X		X			
Viet Nam		X	X	X						
TOTAL	**2**	**3**	**4**	**3**	**3**	**0**	**2**	**1**	**5**	**3**

Source: Freeland and ASEAN WEN research on legal instruments (ASEAN-WEN, Freeland, 2016[14]) .

In contrast to the relatively strong regional framework of treaties, there are fewer agreements in place to facilitate communication and co-ordination between relevant authorities in Southeast Asia and counterparts further afield, however. For example, respondents noted gaps in co-ordination with authorities in sub-Saharan Africa (source countries) and with European (transit and destination) countries. In one case, Indonesian prosecutors from the Attorney General's Office (AGO) indicated that they had received notice of a seized illegal wildlife trade shipment from Indonesia in the Netherlands. However, since Indonesia and the Netherlands currently do not have an established MLAT, authorities were unable to proceed with the full investigation. Authorities in this case have no legal groundwork to request information pertaining to the goods seized as evidence in Europe (Indonesia AGO, 2018[17]).

In Viet Nam, respondents noted that there are liaison officers for the key investigatory agency, the Ministry of Public Safety (MPS) and their customs administration in several sub-Saharan African countries. However, as Viet Nam has not signed any MLATs with the countries in question, the MPS and customs have no legal basis for co-operation in transnational smuggling cases. Respondents also noted that there are relatively few Vietnamese liaison officers located within European (transit) countries, a major transit point for illegal wildlife trade into Asia (IO-1, 2018[27]).

In addition to gaps for legal co-operation, formal information requests suffer from backlogs and significant delays. In a 2013 report on cybercrime, the UN noted that "*the mechanism [of MLATs] is challenged by long response times in practise. Countries reported median response times of 120 days for extradition requests, and 150 days for mutual legal assistance requests, received and sent*" (UN, 2013[32]). In the case of wildlife crime there were no reported uses of MLATs for prosecution of wildlife crimes in the criminal justice pathways in the countries studied.

Officials have also cited concerns of abuse of formal international co-operation for corrupt means. In one case, a senior official cited their experiences with evidence theft once rhino horn was returned back to a source country, which had originally requested the seized wildlife products for a prosecution (GA-3, 2018[33]).

Joint International Investigations

Joint international investigations can be defined as a range of collaborative and co-operative approaches and joint investigative practices (UNODC, 2008[34]). Joint investigations can either be parallel investigations with common goals, or single integrated investigations (UNODC, 2008[34]). These can make employ special investigative techniques such as controlled deliveries, where goods are allowed to transit a country of seizure under close supervision of authorities to identify and arrest additional perpetrators involved in the country of delivery.

The use of joint international investigations is limited in the context of wildlife crime investigations. One respondent noted that no cross-border investigations or controlled deliveries had yet to take place in the focus countries. This stands in relative contrast to other forms of serious organized crimes such as drug smuggling, which have seen co-ordinated responses (IO-1, 2018[27]).

International co-operation among law enforcement

Successful International co-operation among law enforcement can be interpreted as the fruitful interactions and exchanges between relevant law enforcement officials with their counterparts in an international context that lead to investigations, arrests, seizures and prosecutions. In the case of illegal wildlife trade, interactions with a broader and diverse network among relevant countries are likely to bring a positive impact on the capacities to co-ordinate, gather information and intelligence and investigate international criminal syndicates engaged in the illegal wildlife trade.

To co-operate effectively, relevant law enforcement officials may use existing channels hosted by organisations such as INTERPOL (for police) or the World Customs Organisation (WCO) (for customs), or can exchange directly. Informal law enforcement co-operation requires a strong network of relevant officials (connected to CITES and other relevant officers) who have established contact and trust among each other (or through some form of trust-building mechanism) in order to exchange sensitive and useful information pertinent to advancing investigations.

A range of respondents reported successful informal information exchanges between counterpart agencies that led to investigations and prosecutions. Often, such exchanges were reported to have taken place at meetings or workshops and through subsequent follow-up calls and messages once a network had been established (Sinagpore AVA, 2018[24]) (Indonesia National Police, 2018[13]). International co-operation is also reportedly enhanced by non-governmental actors. Law enforcement agencies work closely with NGOs and international organisations, who facilitate contacts among international counterpart agencies at events, or through training seminars or through mutual networks of contacts (ENV Viet Nam, 2018[35]) (WCS Indonesia, 2018[16]). Importantly, respondents noted that trust-building is vital to successful international co-operation for informal exchanges of information (GA-3, 2018[33]) (APCEL, 2018[36]) (INTERPOL,

2018[37]). This level of trust is not only important due to corruption risks, but also to strengthen a mutual understanding of objectives and aims among officials who can offer further assistance and peer-based learning for future cases.

Despite the added-value brought to trafficking investigations from informal co-operation, it remains difficult quantify their impact. While some information exchange platforms (such as those hosted by INTERPOL) do measure the number of messages exchanged (and results), other less formalised exchanges are not reported or recorded.

Regional Dynamics of Co-ordination in Southeast Asia

Indonesia, Singapore, Thailand and Viet Nam are all members of the regional intergovernmental organisation ASEAN. Recent multi-national efforts through the ASEAN forum have focused on wildlife and timber trafficking in the region. A common willingness to increase attention on the topic of illegal wildlife trade has been formalised through recently created ASEAN working structures, including through the regional ASEAN CITES enforcement groups (formerly ASEAN WEN) and the latest ASEAN Senior Officials Meeting on Transnational Crimes (SOMTC).

The ASEAN wildlife Enforcement network (WEN) was created in 2005, and acted as co-ordinating body for illegal wildlife trade within the ASEAN secretariat. The ASEAN WEN was developed through high-level political support to enhance co-ordination among environmental and CITES authorities. The ASEAN WEN secretariat was located in Thailand, and addressed trafficking in illegal wildlife in Asia by reducing consumer demand, strengthening law enforcement and improving regional cooperation and anti-trafficking networks. From 2009-2014, the ASEAN WEN reported over 8,000 cases of illegal wildlife trade seizures and arrests, and noted a tenfold increase in the number of reported wildlife cases. (USAID, 2014[38]). The ASEAN WEN structure was formed with the support of international agencies and partners (such as USAID and Freeland) who assisted in providing funding and training, legal guidance and reviews and expert analyses to help enhance the multi-lateral co-ordination of illegal wildlife trade. In several cases, wildlife enforcement authorities used the ASEAN WEN contact points to exchange and information sharing to conduct independent seizures. For example, Singaporean authorities noted that information received through the ASEAN WEN network was instrumental in the seizure of a large-scale shipment of ivory (Sinagpore AVA, 2018[24]).

Several officials interviewed noted that the ASEAN WEN network was limited in its effectiveness to address and prosecute illegal wildlife trade as a transnational crime. Despite having the subject matter expertise for wildlife crimes, CITES authorities (who remained the primary interlocutors for the ASEAN WEN) generally do not have the institutional capacities or resource to co-ordinate complex investigations involving transnational organized crime. The ASEAN WEN also does not operate a standing task force or series of working groups with set operational plans or objectives (IO-1, 2018[27]) (ENV Viet Nam, 2018[35]). As a result, enforcement efforts like controlled deliveries or joint multi-national investigations are not facilitated through the ASEAN WEN (IO-1, 2018[27]). Operations and investigations which involved international law enforcement co-operation were conducted within parallel informal multi-lateral channels instead: Officials relied on informal networks co-ordinated through on mobile applications (such as WhatsApp) to engage networks for rapid communications between law enforcement contacts (Indonesia MEF, 2018[11]). In 2017, the ASEAN WEN was merged with the ASEAN Experts Group on CITES (AEG) to co-ordinate more closely on the development or a strategic plan with a stronger focus on policy, training and the co-ordination among national wildlife enforcement networks in place across the ASEAN members (CITES, 2017[39]) (Indonesia MEF, 2018[11]) (IO-1, 2018[27]).

Under the leadership of Thailand, the ASEAN Senior Officials Meeting on Transnational Organised Crime (SOMTC) created the Working Group on Illicit Trafficking in Wildlife and Timber in 2018 (GA-3, 2018[33]). Experts have noted that the creation of the SOMTC Working-group marks a shifting perception among governments that illegal wildlife trade is a transnational organised crime (UNODC, 2018[40]). The creation of the SOMTC illegal wildlife trade Working Group highlights how illegal wildlife trade cannot only be handled by environmental and CITES authorities. The addition of illegal wildlife trade to the SOMTC agenda also suggests new opportunities for joint-investigations into international corruption, serious organized crime and potentially money laundering and illicit financial flows[6]. Respondents have noted that the creation of the SOMTC is encouraging, but to ensure the success of this new Working Group, they noted that governments must dedicate more time and resource to building specific targeted strategies and task forces to meet objectives. This can ensure that the SOMTC may become operational beyond the initial design phase (which has been an obstacle in previous iterations of regional illegal wildlife trade efforts) (IO-1, 2018[27]). At the national level in each country, the inclusion of illegal wildlife trade into the agenda also will help improve the profile of this issue among other serious crimes. The ASEAN SOMTC working group on illicit trafficking in wildlife and timber met first in March 2018. The SOMTC continues to involve relevant law enforcement officials and CITES officers in these meetings.

International Dynamics of co-ordination

INTERPOL supports law enforcement agencies in its member countries by facilitating global information sharing on environmental criminal networks and targets, enhancing cooperation among source, transit and destination countries, and building operational capacity within law enforcement agencies.

Box 3.8. INTERPOL Environmental Security Unit

INTERPOL Environmental Security Unit

The INTERPOL Environmental Security Unit consists of four global enforcement teams – focusing mainly on fisheries, forestry, pollution and wildlife crime – that support member countries in dismantling environmental criminal networks. This is done by providing law enforcement agencies with the tools and expertise they need to protect the environment from being exploited by criminals.

The Unit offers investigative support to international environmental criminal cases through an intelligence-led approach, enhancing the sharing of information among countries and the coordination of global operations.

Each INTERPOL member country hosts an INTERPOL National Central Bureau (NCB). This connects their national law enforcement with other countries and with the General Secretariat via our secure global police communications network called I-24/7.

In some instances, respondents pointed to the successful use of INTERPOL contact points and the use of the I-24/7 secure messaging system to exchange information on IWT seizures. For example, Singaporean authorities reported that data and information was fed across INTERPOL NCBs with Vietnamese counterparts in the case of several high-profile ivory and wood seizures in Singapore in route to Viet Nam (Sinagpore AVA, 2018[24]). However, some respondents also noted that the centralized nature of police to police co-operation can discourage the use of INTERPOL systems for the exchange of time-sensitive operational information. According to Experts familiar with international investigations pointed out that the NCBs located within national police headquarters are highly centralized. Resourcing and compatibility issues ("red-tape"), as well as legal considerations remain problematic. Therefore, wildlife crime is not given significant priority for police to police co-operation (IE-1, 2019[41]). Consequently, respondents noted that INTERPOL remains under-used for the purposes of IWT co-operation for investigations and enforcement. Instead, officials rely on personal networks of contacts, liaising through applications such as WhatsApp for rapid exchanges of information and details (Indonesia National Police, 2018[13]).

Conclusion

This chapter provided a review of the institutional capacities in each focus country to leverage multi-agency co-ordination in the effort to deter or combat the illegal wildlife trade. From the research conducted, Thailand is the only country that has made use of its multi-agency task force, the Thailand Wildlife Enforcement Network (WEN), to counter illegal wildlife trade. This WEN has led to several successful enforcement actions against networks of traffickers, notably cases that have involved the financial investigation, asset seizure and forfeiture for transnational criminal networks. Despite the recent successes, the use of the WEN, remains infrequent. In the case of the other focus countries, researchers found no evidence of multi-agency co-operation leading successful investigations: Across the four countries of focus, the vast majority of wildlife crimes involving transnational networks, money laundering and other crimes in the region (including corruption related offenses) do not involve upstream of downstream investigations. Consequently, the primary means of producing evidence for convictions continues to be catching criminals in the act. All of the focus countries are reliant on predicate offenses of wildlife trafficking or trading in endangered species.

This chapter also examined the role of international law enforcement co-operation in enhancing institutional capacities to counter illicit trade. There are a number of formalized arrangements in place between the various ASEAN members, including Mutual Legal Assistance treaties (MLATs) and extradition arrangements between the regional members. In addition, there are a number of newly formed networks for the informal (non-MLAT) co-operation, including the ASEAN Senior Officials Meeting on Transnational Crime (SOMTC) working group on illicit trafficking in wildlife and timber, and the ASEAN Experts Group on CITES. The former, the SOMTC, offers new opportunities for stronger multi-agency investigations at the international level, and the latter, an experts group between CITES management authorities, can offer better co-ordination for policy development and awareness among wildlife authorities of the multi-national dimension of wildlife crime.

Between relevant counterparts in police or CITES authorities, respondents also noted a growing level of informal co-ordination and co-operation for sharing of information. A number of recent cases have involved regional communication and co-ordination, particularly in scenarios where illegal wildlife trade may be intercepted in-transit towards another ASEAN member country. However, as this chapter has also noted, there are fewer multi-national instances of co-operation for countries further afield in source or transit countries across Southern and Eastern Africa or Europe.

Few legal arrangements are in place between law enforcement agencies in the region and law enforcement in source countries to formally exchange information. Contact points between African and Southeast Asian law enforcement counterparts are not well developed when it comes to combatting the illegal wildlife trade. Vital channels of police to police exchange and communication between source and transit economies from Africa to Southeast Asia are largely unused due to inefficiencies, compatibility issues and long response times. Furthermore, there is a notable breakdown in institutional co-ordination, and absence of trusted counterparts for cases involving southern and eastern African countries. Respondents also pointed to corruption risks and lack of contact as reasons for breakdowns in correspondence and co-ordination.

The findings from this chapter point to a greater need for multi-agency co-ordination at the national level and at the international level to ensure the success of complex upstream and downstream investigations. To achieve this, governments may wish to consider developing strategic action plans or roadmaps outlining specific targets, and outlining the relevant agencies' roles and responsibilities, and measurable performance indicators for countering illegal wildlife trade. There is also a need to establish more effective professional networks of law-enforcement officials across continents in source, transit and destination countries that can find suitable alternatives when formal processes for law enforcement exchanges are moving too slowly. There is also a need to establish a number of MLATs between these same countries to foster the exchange of formal evidence in support of prosecutions.

References

ACRES (2019), *The Situation in Singapore*, https://acres.org.sg/wildlife-crime/the-illegal-wildlife-trade-singaporeasia/the-situation-in-singapore/ (accessed on 1 February 2019). [21]

ACRES (2018), *In-person interviews with ACRES foundation (multiple), June-August, 2018.* [22]

APCEL (2018), *Meeting with Asia-Pacific Center for Environmental Law, Faculty of Law, National University of Singapore, October 16, 2018.* [36]

ASEAN-WEN, Freeland (2016), *ASEAN Handbook on Legal Cooperation to Combat Illegal Wildlife Trade.* [14]

CFR (2019), *What Is Extradition? Council on Foreign Relations*, https://www.cfr.org/backgrounder/what-extradition (accessed on 24 April 2019). [31]

CITES (2017), *Asean working group on cites and wildlife enforcement (awg cites-wen).* [39]

ENV Viet Nam (2018), *Interview with Education for Nature (ENV), Hanoi, Vietnam, August 20, 2018.* [35]

EU (2016), "EU Action Plan against Wildlife Trafficking (COM(2016) 87 final) Environment", http://dx.doi.org/10.2779/016138. [4]

FD-7 (2018), *Interview with members of Foreign Delegation in Singapore, October 16, 2018.* [23]

Freeland (2018), *Interviews with Freeland (multiple), Bangkok Thailand, July 2018.* [7]

GA-3 (2018), *Interview with Government Agency 3, Bangkok, Thailand, August 23, 2018.* [33]

IE-1 (2019), *Confidential Interview with Independent Expert.* [41]

Indonesia AGO (2018), *In person interview at the Office of the Attorney General: Special Task Force on Natural Resources,October 18, 2018.* [17]

Indonesia Customs (2018), *Interview with the Directorate General of Customs, Ministry of Finance, October 18, 2018.* [10]

Indonesia KPK (2018), *Interview with Indonesia Corruption Eradication Commission (KPK), October 19, 218.* [20]

Indonesia MEF (2018), *Interview with Indonesia Directorate General for Law Enforcement, Ministry of Environment and Forestry, October 17, 2018.* [11]

Indonesia National Police (2018), *Interview with Indonesia National Police, Special Directorate, Illegal Wildlife Trade, October 19, 2018.* [13]

Indonesia PPATK (2018), *Interview with Indonesia Financial Transactions Reports and Analysis Center (PPATK), October 19, 2018.* [12]

INTERPOL (2018), *Interview with Interpol NCB, Bangkok, Thailand 06 July 2018.* [37]

INTERPOL (2013), *National Enviromental Security Task Force (NEST)*, https://www.interpol.int/en/content/download/5100/file/National%20Environmental%20Security%20Task%20Force%20%28NEST%29.pdf (accessed on 25 April 2019). [5]

IO-1 (2018), *Interview with Inter-Governmental Organisation 1, August 20, 2018.* [27]

NG-03 (2018), *Interview with NGO 3 in Sngapore, October 2018.* [25]

OECD (2018), *Strengthening Governance and Reducing Corruption Risks to Tackle Illegal Wildlife Trade: Lessons from East and Southern Africa*, Illicit Trade, OECD Publishing, Paris, https://dx.doi.org/10.1787/9789264306509-en. [1]

Sinagpore AVA (2018), *Interview with Singapore Agriculture and Veterinary Authority, Singapore, October 15, 2018.* [24]

Thailand AMLO (2018), *Interview with Thailand Anti-Money Laundering Authority, Bangkok, Thailand, July 5, 2018.* [6]

TRAFFIC (2018), *Interview with TRAFFIC, Bangkok, Thailand, July 15, 2018.* [8]

UN (2015), *UN Genergal Assembly Resolution Tackling illicit trafficking in wildlifeA/69/L.80 - E - A/69/L.80*, https://undocs.org/A/69/L.80 (accessed on 25 April 2019). [3]

UN (2013), *Comprehensive Study on Cybercrime*, http://www.combattingcybercrime.org/files/virtual-library/national-laws/comprehensive-study-on-cybercrime-%28draft%29.pdf (accessed on 23 April 2019). [32]

UN (2004), *UNITED NATIONS CONVENTION AGAINST TRANSNATIONAL ORGANIZED CRIME AND THE PROTOCOLS THERETO UNITED NATIONS*, http://www.unodc.org (accessed on 18 April 2019). [29]

UNDP (2018), *Interview with UNDP, Jakarta Indonesia, October 18, 2018.* [15]

UNODC (2018), *New regional network to address wildlife and timber trafficking*, https://www.unodc.org/southeastasiaandpacific/en/2018/03/wildlife-somtc/story.html (accessed on 21 December 2018). [40]

UNODC (2015), *Methods of Law Enforcement Cooperation: Tool 4.7 International law enforcement cooperation Overview This tool discusses aspects of international law enforcement cooperation: Channels of law enforcement cooperation Direct bilateral or multilateral contact Cooperation on information-sharing Expanding contacts between investigators Cooperation during investigations*, https://www.unodc.org/documents/human-trafficking/Toolkit-files/08-58296_tool_4-7.pdf (accessed on 14 January 2019). [2]

UNODC (2008), *Draft Informal Expert Working Group On Joint Investigations: Conclusions And Recommendations 2 To 4*, https://www.unodc.org/documents/treaties/COP2008/crp5.pdf (accessed on 24 April 2019). [34]

US DoS (2012), *Treaties and Agreements*, United States Department of State, https://www.state.gov/j/inl/rls/nrcrpt/2012/vol2/184110.htm (accessed on 24 April 2019). [30]

USAID (2014), *Asia's Regional Response to Endangered Species Trafficking*, U.S. Agency for International Development, https://www.usaid.gov/asia-regional/documents/asias-regional-response-endangered-species-trafficking (accessed on 21 December 2018). [38]

Viet Nam MARD (2018), *Interview with Vietnam Minstry of Agriculture and Rural Development, August 21, 2018.* [26]

WCS Indonesia (2018), *Interview with WCS Indonesia offices, October 17, 2018.* [16]

WCS Indonesia (2017), *Wildlife Crimes Unit in Indonesia*, https://rmportal.net/cwt-case-study-compilation/finalists/finalists-pdf-folder/wildlife-crimes-unit-in-indonesia/at_download/file. [18]

WCS WCU (2019), *Wildlife Crimes Unit News Sumatera*, http://www.wildlifecrimesunit.org/News/WCU-Sumatera.aspx. [19]

WildAid (2018), *Ivory Demand In Thailand*, https://wildaid.org/wp-content/uploads/2017/09/Thailand-Survey-EN.pdf (accessed on 22 November 2018). [9]

World Bank (2016), *Project Information Document: Country Vietnam Report*, http://documents.worldbank.org/curated/en/359551484116631137/pdf/SG-PRW-PID-CP-P162792-01-11-2017-1484116624841.pdf (accessed on 18 December 2018). [28]

Notes

[1] In some cases, smugglers have been charged with violations to Law No. 16 year 1992, on animal, fish and plant quarantine. Criminal penalties could take place for the predicate offense of smuggling wildlife products in violation of CITES at border crossings, however no clear evidence suggests that smuggling offenses have led to convictions.

[2] While not formally through any "multi-door" structure, several recent cases have still involved some degree of co-ordination and communication between the MEF, INP and Customs.

[3] Other legislation includes: the Wild Animal and Birds Act, Chapter 351, 1965, revised in 2000 4. Wild Animals (Licensing) Order, 1990, revised in 1992 5. Animals and Birds Act, Chapter 7 [as amended by the Animals and Birds (Amendment) Act No. 46 of 2014

[4] Such scenarios include civil detention where there is no resistance, and for limited periods of time before handover to police.

[5] Under Viet Nam's reformed penal code for the protection of wildlife (Law No. 12/2017/QH14 dated June 20, 2017 of the National Assembly on amending the Criminal Code No.100/2015/QH13), penalties have gone from five years to 15 years, with a penalty of up to USD $600,000 from USD $50,000. These laws came into force January 1, 2018.

[6] Investigations on AML and could take place if investigators liaise effectively with officials within their respective financial intelligence units.

4 Legal frameworks to deter and combat the illegal wildlife trade in Southeast Asia

This chapter discusses domestic and international legal frameworks in place across the four focus countries and within the region. The chapter highlights some of the major gaps in implementation and effectiveness of a number of relevant laws and international conventions necessary to deter criminal syndicates and ensure the adequate protection against illegal wildlife trade and related offenses.

Introduction

Legal Frameworks set forth a set of rules that forbid specific acts and relate these prescriptions to the achievement of clear policy objectives. To prevent, deter and prosecute illegal wildlife trade, governments must implement an effective and comprehensive legal framework. Within such a framework, the institutional arrangements in place must also be organized and co-ordinated in such a manner to hold all persons (public and private) and institutions accountable to these laws, and provide for agency and oversight. The Legal frameworks must reflect the broader international legal standards and norms prescribed through international agreements. Finally, a fully functioning legal framework must be concise and clear, accessible and understood by the public with respect to what actions may be legal or illegal, and avoid overlaps or loopholes that might enable illegal wildlife trade to persist un-punished.

This chapter conducts a review of the various international and domestic legal frameworks in place, and identifies current loopholes and gaps in these frameworks that affect institutional capacities to counter illegal wildlife trade. As this chapter will demonstrate, the various loopholes detailed in this chapter can lead to open markets of illegal wildlife trade, illicit captive breeding schemes, and the 'laundering' of illegal wildlife trade products from illicit markets into grey markets or legal channels.

International Legal Frameworks

A number of relevant international treaties and conventions make up the international legal framework for wildlife crime. This framework enables law enforcement and relevant institutions to harmonize standards, approaches and sets the groundwork for international co-operation on matters related to wildlife crime. International conventions also tie wildlife crime to a range of other criminal offenses (such as corruption, transnational organized crime and others).

In 2018, ASEAN-Wildlife Enforcement Network undertook a legal review of ASEAN countries' respective legislation on wildlife crime. This comprehensive review provides a comparative framework of analysis of relevant laws and their application to countering illegal wildlife trade. The below table summarizes the key findings of this report, highlighting some of the relevant laws with respect to enforcing CITES related laws. As the table below highlights, the countries studied have ratified or acceded to a number of relevant international treaties, including the UN Convention against Corruption, and the UN Convention on Transnational organized crime[1].

Table 4.1. Relevant International Legal Frameworks and tools

Year of Accession

	Indonesia	Singapore	Thailand	Viet Nam
Convention on International Trade in Endangered Species (CITES)	1979	1987	1983	1994
2000 UN Convention on Transnational Organized Crime (UNTOC)	2009	2007	2013	2012
2003 UN Convention Against Corruption (UNCAC)	2006	2007	2011	2009
ASEAN Mutual Legal Assistance for Law Enforcement	2008	Signed not ratified	2013	2008

Source: (ASEAN-WEN, Freeland, 2016[1])

CITES

Each of the four countries are Party to the Convention on International Trade in Endangered Species (CITES), which is the foremost legal framework establishing rules and prohibitions for the trade in endangered fauna (and flora). CITES covers over 5,600 species of Animals. CITES Parties designate an enforcement authority, and regulate the trade and sale in these products through a system of permits and licenses. The four focus countries have CITES Management Authorities that are responsible for permitting and enforcement of aspects relating to the Convention. Regionally, the ASEAN group of nations has also established a recently created an ASEAN CITES enforcement group (formerly ASEAN Wildlife Enforcement Network (WEN). Under CITES, there is no requirement for the harmonization of standards or penalties. Parties must decide on what national controls and penalties are to be implemented to enforce the Convention (i.e. criminal or civil penalties).

The CITES Secretariat co-ordinates annual meetings of the Conference of the Parties (CoP), and the review mechanism for implementation and enforcement of CITES. Reporting standards including notably the CITES annual reports, in addition to reports on national legislation projects, review of significant trade and enforcement matters (CITES, 2012[2])

UNTOC

The Convention on transnational crime is the principle international legal framework for organized crime across borders. The legally binding instrument contains several provisions that require Parties to create of domestic criminal offences in conjunction with international crimes "(participation in an organized criminal group, money laundering, corruption and obstruction of justice); the adoption of frameworks for extradition, mutual legal assistance and law enforcement cooperation; and the promotion of training and technical assistance for building or upgrading the necessary capacity of national authorities" (UNODC, 2000[3]).

There are several protocols of the UNTOC that focus on specific transnational crimes, including human trafficking, illicit arms trafficking, and migrant smuggling. While there are no specific protocols for wildlife crime, Resolution E/2013/30 in the Economic and Social Council of the UN:

> *"Encourages Member States to make illicit trafficking in protected species of wild fauna and flora involving organized criminal groups a serious crime, as defined in article 2, paragraph (b), of the United Nations Convention against Transnational Organized Crime, in order to ensure that adequate and effective means of international cooperation can be afforded under the Convention in the investigation and prosecution of those engaged in illicit trafficking in protected species of wild fauna and flora; (UN, 2013[4])*

The UN resolution also encourages all member states to:

> *"(...)strengthen, where necessary, their national legal and criminal regimes, judicial capacity (...) to ensure that relevant criminal laws including appropriate penalties and sanctions, are available to address illicit trafficking in protected species of wild fauna and flora" (UN, 2013[4]).*

For the purposes of the UNTOC convention, "serious crime" is defined as a crime with a maximum penalty of at least four years. As noted in the overview of the legal framework below, each of the countries, with the exception of Singapore, meets this requirement.

The evaluative framework of the Convention is the Internal Review Mechanism (IRM) which is a peer process, occurring every five years within the secretariat of the UNODC.

UNCAC

The UNCAC is a legally binding international anti-corruption instrument. The Convention covers five key areas: preventive measures, criminalization and law enforcement, international cooperation, asset recovery, and technical assistance and information exchange (UNODC, 2003[5]). The UNCAC sets a series of minimum standards that are to be met under the framework and overseen by a review process.

UNODC notes "corruption is one of the most critical factors facilitating every aspect of wildlife and forest crime." (UNODC, 2019[6]). While not providing any specific items within the text on wildlife crimes, the provisions of the UNCAC stand for all forms of criminality that may be facilitated by corrupt actors. UNCAC provisions can therefore by invoked for the development of a more stringent framework of laws and measures to counter illegal wildlife trade.

The evaluative framework for the UNCAC is the implementation review mechanism, set in 2009 over two five year cycles with two chapters reviewed per-cycle (cycle 1: Chapters III and IV on criminalisation of law enforcement and international co-operation; cycle 2 on chapters II and V on preventive measures and asset recovery). Parties must submit a self-assessment which is submitted for peer review by two other countries. Country visits are not mandatory, and neither is the publication of the integral text for or review by third-parties (U4, 2010[7]).

ASEAN Mutual Legal Assistance for Law Enforcement

All four of the select countries are members of the regional inter-governmental organisation ASEAN, and partake actively in the several working groups under the aegis of the ASEAN Secretariat. ASEAN also co-ordinates regional international frameworks for co-operation, including extradition agreements and Multi-lateral Mutual Legal Assistance Treaties (MLATs).

Assessing the International legal frameworks

International conventions such as CITES, the UNTOC and the UNCAC are legally binding, and ratifying countries must accede to these conventions through the adoption of the provisions by integrating these into national law. In order to achieve the objectives of each international convention, it is first necessary achieve technical compliance with the relevant provisions of these instruments and secondly, to ensure the effectiveness of their implementation. Below is an overview of these two key pillars and the assessment of how legal frameworks are met:

Technical Compliance with International Legal Frameworks

Technical compliance is the implementation of specific requirements under the international legal frameworks that enable a country to satisfy enforceable means, the existence of powers and procedures of competent authorities. These generally comprise the legislative, institutional and supervisory framework in place to meet the standards in a manner consistent with prevailing toolkits and guidelines. The four focus countries of Indonesia, Singapore, Thailand and Viet Nam largely meet the standards of technical compliance with the international legal frameworks (with some reservations). All four countries have ratified the UNTOC, UNCAC and CITES, and have integrated the provisions of these international legal frameworks into domestic laws.

In the case of the UNTOC and the UNCAC, peer-review mechanisms are in place to monitor the uptake of relevant provisions. However these reviews do not contain analyses of crime-specific actions. Therefore, these conventions are not assessed vis-à-vis wildlife crimes in a way to justifiably determine their effectiveness.

Effectiveness of Current Implementation to Stop Wildlife Crime:

The implementation of specific legal provisions in line with international conventions does not guarantee that international legal frameworks will be effective in achieving their intended objective. The effective application of measures determined or guided by these conventions is equally, if not more important, than the simple ratification of conventions and treaties. For example, while the implementation of the MLAT agreement is considered to be met by the ASEAN Agreement to Co-ordinate through Mutual Exchanges of Evidence, the actual effectiveness of this convention is measured in the number of exchanges and subsequent successful prosecutions that have benefitted from evidence received or transmitted through

MLAT requests in a timely manner. Similarly, the UNTOC's effectiveness can be measured by the number of cases that have benefitted from joint investigations and joint operations related to serious transnational organized crime syndicates involved in wildlife trafficking.

The evidence that has been explored in this report suggests that the international conventions in place are largely acceded to and implemented (see table 4.1). For example, with the exception of Singapore, focus countries treat wildlife crime as a serious offense under the UNTOC definition, with maximum penalties in excess of four years (UNODC, 2000[3]). However, responses from interviewees and reviews of the literature suggest that the effectiveness of the international conventions vis-à-vis wildlife crime deterrence, investigation and prosecution is not highly effective. For example, the authors have found that very few corruption and bribery cases have been prosecuted in pursuit of wildlife crimes, and MLAT exchanges are rare and not prioritized for wildlife crime cases. Furthermore, no joint wildlife enforcement operations or investigations have taken place in any of the four countries – a key provision of the UNTOC. While this report has not compiled a systematic assessment of the evidence to determine the effectiveness of international legal frameworks, the below table highlights what such an analysis could compile for indicators of i) implementation ii) effectiveness and iii) evidence to establish a performance metric for the uptake and use of international legal frameworks:

Table 4.2. International Frameworks: Technical Compliance, Effectiveness and Indicators

Below are some examples of technical compliance indicators, and measurements of effectiveness that could be used to assess the overall implementation and use of international legal frameworks:

International Framework	Examples of Indicators of Technical Compliance	Effectiveness Indicators	Example of Measureable:
UNCAC	Establish the following as criminal offenses: -bribery -trading in influence -abuse of functions -illicit enrichment -obstruction of justice	-Bribery and related offenses are effectively investigated during course of investigation into wildlife crime. -Investigations -Officials are prevented from engaging in corrupt practises to commit wildlife related offenses	-Change in the number of bribery or corruption cases related to wildlife crime -Change in the number of investigations of wildlife crimes. -Decrease in reports of corruption related offenses facilitating wildlife crimes, increase in reports of failed attempts at bribery or corrupt practises.
UNTOC	National laws criminalizing: -Organized crime -Obstruction of justice Adoption of measures and frameworks for Mutual legal assistance and cooperation among law enforcement	- International cooperation delivers appropriate information, criminal investigations and prosecution of wildlife crime -Organized crime gangs are charged in multiple jurisdictions. -International criminal syndicates are prevented from entering into the country.	-Number of joint-investigations -Number of Joint operations -Number of successful arrests and prosecutions based on information exchanged from partner law enforcement agency.
CITES	-Adopt a general policy framework to protect endangered species -Take necessary measures for the identification, protection, classification of endangered species -Creation of CITES Management Authorities	-CITES Management authority effectively monitors and regulates wildlife markets and successfully identifies trafficking cases, fraudulent CITES certificates, while working in co-operation with relevant authorities -CITES listed species are interdicted inland and at national entry points	-Number of illegally traded CITES listed species that are successfully identified along illicit trade chain. -Number of fraudulent CITES certificates identified -Number of investigations undertaken or assisted with
ASEAN Mutual Legal Assistance for Law Enforcement	-Signing MLATs between all member countries	-International exchanges of evidence between competent authorities deliver appropriate information and necessary evidence to effectively prosecute wildlife crimes	-Number of exchanges of evidence received and sent -Service standard or average time to process and fulfil MLAT Requests -Number of cases that have relied on information obtained through MLATs

National Legal Frameworks

The legislative framework for illegal wildlife trade in the four focus countries is composed of relevant laws, their implementation and their enforcement. The international legal frameworks highlighted above are implemented by the adoption of relevant corresponding national legislation. Table 4.3 summarizes the relevant national legislation for the implementation of CITES to prohibit the trade of illegal wildlife trade within each country, the penalties, and the implementing authority.

Table 4.3. Key Provisions from Wildlife Laws and Relevant Laws

Provisions, Maximum Sentences and Fines

	Indonesia	Singapore	Thailand	Viet Nam
Criminalization of Wildlife Trafficking	Yes	Yes	Yes	Yes
Length of Penalty	10 years	2 years[2]	7 years	15 years
Principle Legislation for illegal wildlife trade trafficking and/or possession	acts, No.5/1990 on 'Conservation of Living Resources and their Ecosystem', as well as the Government Regulation No. 7/1999, 'Preservation of Plants and Animal Species'	Endangered Species (Import and Export) (Act Chapter 92A, 2006, revised in 2008	Thailand Wildlife and Animal Protection Act as amended B.E. 2557 (2014) (WARPA), Ivory Trade Act B.E. 2558 (2015)	Law No. 12/2017/QH14 dated June 20, 2017 of the National Assembly on amending the Criminal Code No. 100/2015/QH13
Implementing Authority	Ministry of Environment and Forestry	Agriculture and Veterinary Authority	Ministry of Natural Resources and Environment	Ministry of Agriculture, and Rural Development
Wildlife Trafficking a Serious Crime	Yes	No	Yes	Yes
Maximum Penalty ($USD)	790,000	370,000	1,100*	600,000
Criminalisation of Possession of ALL non-native CITES species	No	Yes	No	Yes
Penalty / GDP per Capita Ratio	228	6.7	31	24.5
IWT a predicate offense	Yes	Yes	Yes	Yes
Money Laundering Penalty	20 years	10 years	10 years	15 years
Corruption Offenses (accepting a bribe)	15 years	5 years	Life	Life

Note: * Thailand penalty for Ivory possession is up to 6 million baht, or $USD 181,000 under 2015 Ivory Act.
Source: Freeland, ASEAN-WEN; UNODC; OECD Research; ENV Viet Nam

With the exception of Singapore, the focus countries treat illegal wildlife trade as a serious crime according to the UNODC definition (which stipulates that serious crimes must involve sentences of no less than 4 years)[3]. Penalties for associated crimes, such as money laundering and corruption are greater in duration and monetary fines than the penalties for illegal wildlife trade in all of the countries studied, suggesting that additional punitive tools, particularly asset seizure and civil penalties, are available in the case of wildlife crime. In addition, all of the legal systems studied make additional consideration for transnational organized crime (TNOC) in some way to either increase the length of the penalty or to charge a separate offense (ASEAN-WEN, Freeland, 2016[1]).

It is noteworthy that the implementing authority for relevant wildlife laws is not necessarily the principal enforcement body for illegal wildlife trade along the trade chain. For example, the enforcement of illegal wildlife trade related laws at the border falls to the customs administration to regulate imports. Inland, national or regional police agencies are also tasked with enforcement of relevant wildlife laws or organized criminal activities dealing with illegal wildlife trade. CITES management agencies themselves may also have investigation and enforcement powers, but these are often limited in scope. From this initial overview of legislation, implementation and enforcement, the delegated responsibilities are already spread over a range of institutions, hinting at the institutional challenges that lie ahead for co-ordination, resourcing and capacities.

Legal gaps between implementation and enforcement of laws enable the sale and circulation of illegal wildlife trade

It is noteworthy that both international legal frameworks and national legal frameworks are not a metric for performance in enforcing and prosecuting illegal wildlife trade. The treaties and agreements signed at an international level, and the laws in force in each country are a range of tools (i.e. *de jure)* that are available to relevant authorities to be able to conduct complex investigations and prosecute serious crimes. The actual use of these tools (i.e. de *facto)* is measurable only in number of prosecutions and the length of sentences undertaken using relevant legal frameworks. The OECD could not ascertain the number of relevant cases and prosecutions that have made use of tools or co-ordination under these legal frameworks. There are a number of important barriers and gaps that prevent the effective implementation of such laws and frameworks.

Open Sale and Consumption of Smuggled illegal wildlife trade Products

Legal provisions for the enforcement of CITES that criminalize wildlife trafficking are generally robust in the four countries of focus, but only at the national entry points. In all four countries, it is illegal to smuggle any illegal wildlife trade product as this would contravene customs laws, relevant quarantine laws and CITES laws with clearly ban the trade in endangered species without a permit. However, once the illegal wildlife trade product is successfully smuggled into the country by criminal networks, a number of factors come into play that can pose challenges for enforcing wildlife laws, and the legal framework is considerably weaker due to gaps between implementation and enforcement. Interviews undertaken by the OECD researchers, analysis of relevant laws and supporting research suggests that there are a range of obstacles that prevent the full implementation of these laws.

In the four countries studied, discussions with experts and relevant agencies confirm that there are extensive legal and grey markets for a range of wildlife products that fall under CITES Appendix I (the most endangered under CITES categories of species). These legal markets offer opportunities for criminal elements to "launder" illegally killed or taken animals into a parallel legal market. An overview of the practical implementation of laws suggests that authorities are restricted in the use of relevant national legislation which leads to a complex and potentially conflicting interpretation of laws which prevents effective and practical enforcement.

In Thailand, and Indonesia, CITES Appendix I, II and III species are only subject to relevant controls at national border. Within the economy, wildlife officials have not criminalized the keeping of CITES species unless they are contained on a list of nationally recognized endangered species. In Thailand, this separate list is prescribed under the Thailand Wildlife and Animal Protection Act (WARPA) (see example below). In Indonesia, the internal trade and sale of wildlife is regulated by Government Regulation No. 7/1999, 'Preservation of Plants and Animal Species'. In both these cases, the national laws do not explicitly criminalize non-endemic endangered wildlife for sale and possession, which contributes to large thriving markets for endangered species (see examples below).

Box 4.1. Laundering' of Illegal Wildlife Products

Thailand's Markets for Exotic Pets and Animals thrive off legal loopholes

In Thailand, legal gaps offer ambiguity on the status of endangered species that are trafficked against international conventions. Chattuchak Market next to Bangkok is one of the best-known examples of the open and legal trade in endangered animals. Markets such as this one are recognized as a global hub for illegal wildlife trade in the region, and also as a market for illegal wildlife trade consumed as far as Europe and the United States (UNDP, 2017[8]).

According to the Thailand Wildlife and Animal Protection Act as amended B.E. 2557 (2014) (WARPA), CITES controlled species are not protected unless specified on a list of endangered species prescribed Department of National Parks and Wildlife (DNPW). This DNPW administered list of "protected" species contains only 12 non-native endangered species (UNODC, 2017[9]). All non-listed endangered species can therefore be sold in markets (since there are no practical means to provide evidence that these animals were not captive-bred). Experts have noted that these loopholes not only create a large market for illegal wildlife trade, but also offers strong incentives for smugglers to bring illegal wildlife trade across the Thai border and into the economy (GA-3, 2018[10]).

Indonesia's legal loopholes allow the trade of non-native CITES products

The acts, No.5/1990 on 'Conservation of Living Resources and their Ecosystem', as well as the Government Regulation No. 7/1999, 'Preservation of Plants and Animal Species' define the conditions for the legal and illegal keeping of wildlife, and how a list of protected species is determined, respectively. According to these laws, consultations with scientific authorities and a Ministerial decree specify which animals are on such a list. To-date, non-native species are not featured on this list. This legal loophole allows the trade of any non-endemic animal poached illegally abroad. The sale of foreign poached illegal wildlife trade trafficked In Indonesia's markets is documented by the wildlife NGO TRAFFIC. For example, surveys of species of turtles and tortoises for sale in Jakarta's markets found that non-native species made up 77% of all animals advertised (TRAFFIC, 2018[11]). The species of turtles and tortoises observed came from Africa, Asia, Europe, Madagascar, and North and South America. Nearly half of the species observed were categorized as near extinction, and several featured on CITES Appendix I, indicating that international trade is prohibited without certificates.

Early in 2018, the government launched a revision of the Natural Resources Conservation Law of 1990 (No.5/1990). Some aspects of the draft law target illegal wildlife trade more effectively – such as banning the trade in species regulated by CITES. However, the law also purportedly weakens other existing provisions, such as the new self-defence clause that waives criminal charges for killing protected wildlife. The law offers what critics say is a less clear definition of wildlife crime that could make it harder to crack down on traffickers (Gokkon, 2018[12]).

The gaps between implementation and the enforcement of laws is particularly visible in the case of the ivory trade. In the four focus countries, ivory can be considered legal if it is "vintage" (pre-CITES) or sourced from legal stocks. While ivory can be tested for age by systems that include carbon dating (APCEL, 2018[13]) there are no practical verification methods available on a cost-effective basis that enable the rapid differentiation between ivory that may be classified as legal or illegal (GA-3, 2018[10]). A number of examples below highlight the way in which the loopholes and gaps facilitate the sale of illegal wildlife trade products throughout all of the economies in the region.

Box 4.2. The Legal and Open Trade of Ivory Across Southeast Asia

Thailand's Domesticated Elephant Ivory Trade

Thailand is home to about 43,000 wild forest elephants, and approximately 1,250 domesticated tusk-bearing elephants. The latter are used for tourism purposes and moving heavy objects, and are subject to a different set of wildlife laws. For example, the animals themselves, and the ivory from domesticated "beasts of burden" can be bought and sold openly for commercial trade purposes if it has been registered with the DPNW.

Prior to 2015, all ivory goods purported to be from beasts of burden could be marketed and sold openly without necessary documentation. This resulted in the widespread open sale of illegal ivory products. A 2014 survey in Bangkok identified over 14,000 pieces of ivory for sale in open markets in over 100 retail storefronts. Meanwhile, "the maximum quantity of ivory that the country's domesticated elephants could produce is estimated at 650 kg annually, a quantity that is considerably less than what was observed in Bangkok markets" (TRAFFIC, 2014[14]). The Ivory Trade Act B.E. 2558 (2015) introduced a number of provisions to regulate the domestic ivory market. The Act criminalizes the sale of wild domestic or foreign African elephants and elephant products. Under the new law, all existing elephant ivory must be registered under a reporting scheme, and any new ivory sold must be accompanied by proof of provenance.

Since the implementation of the 2015 Ivory Trade Act, the number of ivory products openly for sale had fallen from 14,000 to an average of 2,000 by 2016 (TRAFFIC, 2016[15]). The 2015 Act is a step forward in closing one of the loopholes that allow the sale of illegal ivory products. However, a number of risks persist, namely sales in other marketplaces, such as online sales and in informal networks of buyers and sellers.

Open Ivory Markets in Singapore

In 2016, the wildlife NGO WWF set up a website in purporting to sell a wide variety of ivory pieces to a Singaporean clientele. Reactions to the website included widespread condemnation. However, as the wildlife NGO later pointed out, the domestic sale of ivory online would have in fact been legal. Under existing laws, if ivory is claimed to be "vintage" or pre-CITES (i.e. imported into Singapore before 1990), it can be openly bought and sold in Singapore. Indeed, according to one recent survey, ivory was openly sold in 40 storefronts across Singapore and is available for purchase online (WWF, 2018[16]).

Given that there are no distinguishing features or systems to quickly analyse or date ivory without professional forensic investigation techniques, the open and unregulated sale of "vintage" ivory creates important gaps that can enable the trafficking of illegally obtained, recently killed elephant ivory. Furthermore, there are no official statistics on the stock of pre-CITES ivory, and it is not possible to assess what quantity of ivory could be *bona fide* "vintage" and what quantity has been illegally imported and sold (WWF, 2018[16]).

Captive breeding and the trade in live animals in illegal zoos

In the case of domestically occurring wildlife, one of the main concerns raised by respondents related to the illegal killing of protected wildlife, which is then exported live, or in parts and pieces. Respondents raised questions over the existing legal and regulatory frameworks that define the capture, farming and consumption of animal parts from zoos, farms, sanctuaries and other captive schemes.

Several cases were raised where wildlife traffickers in the region used licensing schemes for zoos, farms and wildlife sanctuaries. In several of the countries studied, criminals obtain permits, often through legal means, and then abuse these schemes to sell wildlife into black markets. Animals involved include domestically occurring species, but also internationally trafficked animals. For example, Asian big-cats (such as tigers) and bears are bred across Southeast Asia, and are sold into exotic pet trades or farmed for animal parts (Thailand AMLO, 2018[17]) (ENV Viet Nam, 2018[18]). In other cases, illegally imported animals such as tortoises are smuggled into farms to masquerade as domestically farmed when they are in fact poached from the wild (UNODC, 2017[9]).

Box 4.3. Zoos and Sanctuaries Facilitating the illegal wildlife trade

Fewer than 4,000 tigers remain in the wild, but as many as 8,000 are in captivity across Laos, China, Cambodia, Thailand and Viet Nam (Stoner et al., 2016[19]). A number of zoos and facilities in the region are licensed to operate for educational and research purposes, but responses from experts and previous research and investigations suggest that these schemes are being abused across the region. These farms feed a strong demand for tiger parts as a luxury good and for traditional medicines (Thailand NACC, 2018[20]) (National Geographic, n.d.[21]) .

Research on tiger farms across the region suggests that many of these captive breeding facilities are part of a wider chain of illegal wildlife trade and smuggling networks and some of the tigers in such facilities are in fact laundered wild-caught animals. Many of the big cats in the captive breeding zoos or sanctuaries are then killed and smuggled throughout the region to feed consumption among other South East Asian countries, including China and Viet Nam (WJC, 2016[22]).

The "grey market" loophole for tiger farming in Viet Nam

In Viet Nam, owning a tiger and trafficking is a criminal offense under the penal code. However, the law governing captive breeding, the 'Decree of Management of Export, Import, Transit, Breeding and Artificial Propagation of Rare, Endangered Wild Fauna and Flora' (Decree 82/2006/ND-CO), enables possession with a license. Provisions of this law require persons to register with the CITES authority, MARD. MARD may delegate responsibility for oversight to provincial and municipal levels.

The Provisions of the Decree on Management of Endangered, Precious and Rare Species (Decree No. 32/02006/ND-CP), stipulates the conditions for breeding of animals, particularly critically endangered species:

"Exploitation of endangered, precious and rare forest plants and animals of (CITES) Group I (...) shall be exploited only for scientific purposes of research"

However, the law also notes that:

"It is permitted to process or trade (...) for commercial purposes: endangered, precious and rare forest animal species originating from artificial breeding, and products thereof."

The decrees above illustrate the legal provisions which restrict but also permit commercial legal trade in captive-bred CITES Category I species. This provides an important incentive for illegal wildlife trade traffickers to obtain such licenses and maintain these under false pretences other than "scientific research".

Respondents cited several examples of the abuse of these "grey areas" under such existing laws for the licensing schemes. For example respondents highlighted a case where the spouse of a convicted high-level wildlife trafficker is in possession of a license to keep over a dozen tigers for a "conservation and education" (ENV Viet Nam, 2018[18]). One other responding organisation argued that this particular case highlighted how the MARD process of granting licenses was effectively an administrative step that was undertaken without cooperation with other agencies or consideration of the resources needed to conduct necessary verifications (IO-1, 2018[23]).

Legislative reforms and amendments

In December 2018, the Singapore government held a public consultation to introduce a total ban on the sale of ivory, which would potentially also include pre-CITES pieces (WildAid, 2018[24]). A similar ban has been considered and discussed in Viet Nam as well.

Early in 2018, the government launched a revision of the Natural Resources Conservation Law of 1990. Some aspects of the draft law target illegal wildlife trade more effectively – such as banning the trade in species that are regulated by CITES, the main international treaty on endangered animals and plants. However, it also purportedly weakens the existing law, such as the new 'self-defence' clause that waives criminal charges for killing protected wildlife. A less clear definition of wildlife crime that could make it harder to crack down on traffickers.

Thailand has amended the Ivory Act to integrate a mechanism of verification and regulation that closes a gap on the open sale and display of ivory products without appropriate documentation. The ivory act amendment is noted to be effective in the reduction of listed illegal wildlife trade products. However, the regulation of the sale of ivory does not prevent the open wearing and display of ivory products. As noted by one official, "telling the difference between African and Asian elephant's ivory, once it is carved is next to impossible" (GA-3, 2018[10]). The impact of this reform be limited as goods may be illegally imported and sold on other networks, including in thriving online marketplaces. There are also further complications with respect to documentation requirements for the export of ivory, which is not covered by the reformed Act. (GA-3, 2018[10]).

Legal Markets Put Added Pressure on National Entry Points:

In all four countries studied, there are only partial bans on the sale of ivory. Therefore, there are strong incentives to ensure that illegal wildlife trade products enter the economy into relatively free circulation. The stark contrast between border enforcement and free inner-market mobility can create a choke point dynamic for illegal wildlife trade products. This leads to even greater strain and pressure on customs officials and other relevant officials posted along border checkpoints, airports and seaports to detect and target illegal wildlife trade, among an already long-list of other contraband products that must be identified (e.g. narcotics, counterfeits, customs fraud, etc.). This adds to a risk that border crossings become a corruption and smuggling hot-spot for traffickers who will dedicate more resources and attempt to co-opt or corrupt officials with larger sums to gain entry into the country (as the goods are "home-free" once smuggled in). As explored in greater depth in the chapter on corruption and illegal wildlife trade, this same pressure also applies to persons employed privately and other officials with authorities at crossing points.

Conclusions

At first glance, in the four countries studied, the international legal framework and national laws put in place harsh penalties and high monetary fines. In all but one case, wildlife trafficking alone is a serious crime. However, illegal wildlife trade related laws could be circumvented with relative ease by criminal networks with the right means and resources. Several of the cases highlighted above illustrate how legal loopholes can be abused for domestic consumption of CITES listed species and for facilitating the transfer of animals into the broader illegal wildlife trade supply chain in the region. For example, the abuse of licensing schemes for farms creates a necessary parallel legal market, which not only facilitates the illegal production of illegal wildlife trade, but also offers the social acceptability of wearing, display and consumption of illegal wildlife trade parts that actually come from poached or illegally farmed animals. As this chapter has also explored, these gaps, oversights and challenging enforcement scenarios put a number of increased pressures on officials posted at national entry-points, and help to maintain illegal wildlife trade as a low-risk, high reward crime.

Recently amended laws, such as those increasing penalties and registering and restricting sale and possession of certain products highlight a changing attitude within the region on the open sale of wildlife products (particularly ivory). However, proposed reforms still fall short of closing a number of legal loopholes and gaps in enforceability. For example, in several cases, experts have advocated for product marking schemes and the use of forensic identification tools to ensure that the legally marketed products are *bona fide* (GA-3, 2018[10]) (Indonesia AGO, 2018[25]). The impact of forensic testing for ivory would be limited to only one form of illegal wildlife trade (ivory) and would not address the broader legal loopholes for other products. Product marking schemes would be challenging, as a single piece of ivory can be carved, re-shaped and broken-down into hundreds of individual pieces, suggesting that this undertaking would be nearly impossible without significant investment and innovation. These findings suggest that broader reforms to laws and regulations, as well as enforcement frameworks are necessary.

References

APCEL (2018), *Meeting with Asia-Pacific Center for Environmental Law, Faculty of Law, National University of Singapore, October 16, 2018.* [13]

ASEAN-WEN, Freeland (2016), *ASEAN Handbook on Legal Cooperation to Combat Illegal Wildlife Trade.* [1]

CITES (2012), *CITES Compliance andEnforcement Regime.* [2]

ENV Viet Nam (2018), *Interview with Education for Nature (ENV), Hanoi, Vietnam, August 20, 2018.* [18]

GA-3 (2018), *Interview with Government Agency 3, Bangkok, Thailand, August 23, 2018.* [10]

Gokkon, B. (2018), *Environmental Advocates Take Aim at Proposed Revisions to Indonesia's Conservation Act - Pacific Standard*, Pacific Standard, https://psmag.com/environment/new-criticism-of-indonesia-conservation-law (accessed on 13 December 2018). [12]

Indonesia AGO (2018), *In person interview at the Office of the Attorney General: Special Task Force on Natural Resources,October 18, 2018.* [25]

IO-1 (2018), *Interview with Inter-Governmental Organisation 1, August 20, 2018.* [23]

Nam, E. (2016), *The Penal Code Revision: A wildlife protection milestone for Vietnam*, http://www.envietnam.or (accessed on 27 November 2018). [26]

National Geographic (n.d.), *Exclusive Investigation Shows Tiger Farms Linked to Trafficking in Southeast Asia*, 2018, https://www.nationalgeographic.com/animals/2018/07/wildlife-watch-news-captive-tiger-farms-trafficking-investigation-vietnam-laos/ (accessed on 30 November 2018). [21]

Stoner, S. et al. (2016), *Reduced to Skin and Bone: An analysis of Tiger seizures from 13 range countries from 2000-2015*, http://d2ouvy59p0dg6k.cloudfront.net/downloads/reduced_to_skin_and_bones_re_examined_full_analysis.pdf (accessed on 11 December 2018). [19]

Thailand AMLO (2018), *Interview with Thailand Anti-Money Laundering Authority, Bangkok, Thailand, July 5, 2018.* [17]

Thailand NACC (2018), *Interview with Thailand National Anti-corruption Commission, July 5, 2018.* [20]

TRAFFIC (2018), *Slow and Steady: The Global Footprint of Jakarta's Tortoise and Freshwater Turtle Trade*, http://static1.1.sqspcdn.com/static/f/157301/27865373/1521988425807/Jakartas-Tortoise-and-Freshwater-turtle-trade-web.pdf?token=pcanRKCjUQWp67U%2FakdZK5EB%2BzA%3D (accessed on 29 November 2018). [11]

TRAFFIC (2016), *In Transition: Bangkok's Ivory Market An 18-month survey of Bangkok's ivory market*, http://www.trafficj.org/publication/16_In_Transition_Bangkok's_Ivory_Market.pdf (accessed on 28 November 2018). [15]

TRAFFIC (2014), *Polishing off the Ivory: Surveys of Thailand's Ivory Market*, https://www.traffic.org/site/assets/files/8410/thailand-market-survey-report.pdf (accessed on 28 November 2018). [14]

U4 (2010), *UNCAC in a nutshell: A quick guide to the United Nations Convention against Corruption for embassy and donor agency staff*, https://www.cmi.no/publications/file/3769-uncac-in-a-nutshell.pdf. [7]

UN (2013), *E/RES/2013/40: Crime prevention and criminal justice responses to illicittrafficking in protected species of wild fauna and flora*, https://www.unodc.org/documents/commissions/CCPCJ/Crime_Resolutions/2010-2019/2013/ECOSOC/Resolution_2013-40.pdf. [4]

UNDP (2017), *Combating Illegal Wildlife Trade, focusing on Ivory, Rhino Horn, Tiger and Pangolin in Thailand.* [8]

UNODC (2019), *Corruption and wildlife and forest crime*, https://www.unodc.org/unodc/en/corruption/wildlife-and-forest-crime.html. [6]

UNODC (2017), *Criminal justice response to wildlife crime in Thailand: A Rapid Assessment*, http://www.dariopignatelli.com/ (accessed on 8 November 2018). [9]

UNODC (2003), *United Nations Convention against Corruption*, https://www.unodc.org/unodc/en/corruption/tools_and_publications/UN-convention-against-corruption.html. [5]

UNODC (2000), *UN Convention on Transnational Organized Crime.* [3]

WildAid (2018), *Singapore Government Proposes Ban on Sale of Elephant Ivory*, https://wildaid.org/singapore-government-proposes-ban-on-sale-of-elephant-ivory/ (accessed on 30 November 2018). [24]

WJC (2016), *Operation Ambush*, https://wildlifejustice.org/wp-content/uploads/2018/08/WJC-Ambush-Briefing-Public.pdf (accessed on 30 November 2018). [22]

WWF (2018), *Interview with WWF, Singapore, October 16, 2018.* [16]

Notes

[1] Singapore has not ratified the relevant ASEAN MLAT or the FATF treaty.

[2] In Singapore, although recent legal reforms have enhanced the financial penalties from IWT from a maximum of USD $36,000 to over $360,000 and up to two years in jail, some argue that these penalties remain insufficient to effectively deter IWT trafficking, This is particularly the case for high volume, or high value products such as ivory or rhino products, or other environmental crimes involving forestry products, whose value can exceed tens of millions of dollars.

[3] In Viet Nam, as of January 2018 the penal code was amended, increasing the penalties for conviction of IWT related offenses from 7 years to 15 years and new fines up to $USD 600,000 (Nam, 2016[26]).

5 Corruption Risks and the Illegal Wildlife Trade

This chapter discusses the corruption risks that facilitate the illegal wildlife and institutional responses. The chapter outlines some of the national approaches to corruption and illegal wildlife trade in the focus countries, and offers several specific examples of corruption risks and vulnerabilities. The chapter concludes that there is a need to strengthen anti-corruption efforts to address the illegal wildlife trade in the focus countries, drawing upon examples of corruption cases for environmental crimes (such as corruption related to forestry crimes).

Introduction

Corruption[1] undermines the rule of law, erodes quality of life, distorts markets and threatens human security. In response to this persistent and high-level risk, a number of practical tools have been developed by the international community. The OECD Public Governance policy community has developed several important OECD Instruments in this area, including the 2017 OECD Council Recommendation on Public Integrity, updating an earlier instrument, and the 2003 OECD Council Recommendation on Managing Conflicts of Interest in the Public Service. These instruments provide a strategic perspective to frame a discussion on public integrity, including how to fight corruption that acts as a facilitator of illicit trade.

The findings detailed in this chapter echo several of the findings from the 2018 OECD report. The dearth of substantive quantitative data or a wide baseline of convictions poses the most significant challenge to study. In all but one of the countries studied[2], corruption is a critical enabler of the importation of illegal wildlife trade into end-user markets. These findings also highlight once again that there is a clear and pressing need to address corruption as part of intensive international efforts to counter illegal wildlife trade.

International Responses to Corruption

A number of important strides have been made in the anti-corruption discourse. Whereas fifteen years ago, this topic was completely left-off of the policy discussion, it occupies a more and more central role in international approaches to wildlife crime. Today, several high-level policy outcomes have explicitly recognized corruption as an enabler of illegal wildlife trade that must be addressed. For example, United National General Assembly (UNGA) Resolutions of 2015 and 2017 on tackling illicit trafficking in wildlife specifically mention corruption as an underlying enabler of wildlife crime (UN, 2017[1]) (UN, 2015[2]). Furthermore, several state-led processes have also sought to tackle corruption. This has included the 2014 and 2018 London Conferences on Illegal Wildlife Trade; the African Union Strategy "Combatting Illegal Exploitation and Illegal Trade in Fauna and Flora in Africa" (AU, 2015[3]); and the EU's "Action Plan against Wildlife Trafficking" (EU, 2016[4]). Multi-lateral fora such as the G20 have also issued specific statements in recognition of the role of corruption as a facilitator of the illegal wildlife trade in the 2017 "G20 High Level Principles on Combatting Corruption Related to Illegal Trade in Wildlife and Wildlife Products" (G20, 2017[5]). Finally, CITES' 2017 resolution (Conf. 17.6) is specifically dedicated to "Prohibiting, preventing, detecting and countering corruption, which facilitates activities conducted in violation of the Convention". The corruption risks included in this CITES report relate to:

- Bribery to obtain permits for export or collection or trade-restricted species;
- Knowingly overlooking or authorisation false information on permits for export of trade-restricted species, (e.g.: animals collected from the wild exported as captive-bred)
- Sentencing anomalies in the courts
- Tampering with evidence
- Leakage from stockpiles

In addition to high-level anti-corruption statements and policy guidance on this topic, a number of tools have also been developed. These include the UNODC Analytic Toolkits on Wildlife and Forest Crime (UNODC, 2015[6]), the WWF and TRAFFIC primer on wildlife crime and corruption (WWF/TRAFFIC, 2015[7]) as well as the ongoing development of a UNODC Integrity Guide for Wildlife Management Authorities (forthcoming). USAID is also funding a new consortium entitled "Targeting Natural Resource Corruption", led by WWF to capture existing anti-corruption knowledge, generate new evidence and best practises against corruption; make learning available to practitioners; and test strategic approaches on the ground to wildlife crime.

In support of providing additional evidence to this policy issue in source and transit countries, the 2018 OECD publication '*Strengthening Governance and Reducing Corruption Risks to Tackle Illegal Wildlife Trade'* also provided a preliminary insight into the impact of corruption as a facilitator and enabler of illegal wildlife trade in source and transit countries. The report notes that corruption's forms are diverse and dynamic, evolving in line with their specific institutional and supply chain factors (OECD, 2018[8]). The report's findings also detail that no corruption cases had taken place over the five year period studied within the four focus countries, despite widespread acknowledgment that corruption risks were a key facilitator of wildlife crime within the region.

Despite the growing recognition that corruption is a facilitator of wildlife crime, few arrests or prosecutions are known to have taken place to actually target corrupt actors facilitating illegal wildlife trade and other related crimes.

Corruption risks as facilitators of the illegal wildlife trade

The focus on corruption *risks* is important. Indeed, the dearth of large-scale quantitative data and the lack of a wide baseline of convictions has limited the research conducted for this chapter. In this context, through a combination of interviews conducted, data collection and literature reviews, the OECD has employed empirical evidence to develop a framework for identifying corruption risks in Southeast Asia. The chapter also draws on alternative methods: alongside a review of relevant, existing publications and open-source media mapping exercise, it harnesses the first-hand experience of those charged with responding to illegal wildlife trade on the ground. Due to the anecdotal nature of their insights, the purpose of this report is to outline known risks from corruption, as opposed to quantifying confirmed instances of corrupt activity on a large scale. The below table summarizes the various references to corruption risks raised by the numerous respondents throughout OECD interviews, and in the existing literature, alongside the relevant agencies or ministries that are affected.

Table 5.1. Identified References to Corruption along the illegal wildlife trade Value Chain in Southeast Asia and Relevant Agency Mentioned

	Wildlife / Forestry Rangers	CITES authority officers	Police Officers	Customs	Airport Officials / Security	Investigators (police)	Magistrates
Corruption Risks in the Wildlife Trade Chain							
Direct assistance to poachers or poaching[3]	X		X				
Passive assistance to poachers[4]	X	X					
Theft from stockpiles		X	X				
Assisting traffickers to allow entry of illegal wildlife trade into country		X[5]	X	X	X		
Corruption Risks in Licensing and Permit Schemes							
Granting permits under false or fraudulent pretences		X					
Corruption Risks in the Criminal Justice Pathway							
Not enforcing illegal wildlife trade laws in marketplaces		X	X				
Intentional gaps in investigation						X	
Lenient Sentencing/Fines							X

Source: OECD Interviews and Research

Table 5.2. Confirmed Corruption Cases Identified by OECD over past 10 years

Total known cases identified that have involved corruption investigations by national anti-corruption agencies or charges in connection to acts of corruption

Country	Case	Year	Outcome
Viet Nam	Customs Officer arrested and charged with embezzlement after theft from stock rooms of seized ivory products	2018	Conviction for embezzlement -16 years
Thailand	NACC investigation into state officer who secured the issuance after National Park officers arrested in protected animal carcasses,	n/a	N/a
Thailand	Customs officer investigated for after rhino horn and ivory were stolen from a stockpile;	2011	n/a
Thailand	Prosecution of Thai Science and Technology Minister over abuse of authority, from decision to export over 100 Bengal tiger carcasses. Minister found 'not guilty' because the export was endorsed by the Director General of the Department of National Parks.	2012	Not-guilty
Thailand	Senior official arrested in connection to wildlife poaching in national park	2018	n/a

Source: OECD interviews and research.

Literature Review and Open Media Mapping

The OECD undertook a literature review on the topic of corruption in relation to illegal wildlife trade in the countries studied. In summary, this literature review found that there is considerably less research on this topic in the whole region in comparison to the previous East African project, which found that over 100 articles reported on this issue. The OECD found approximately only 20 reports of direct relevance to this research. Of these reports, four focus on the region as a whole, whereas the others focus on national or sub-regional dynamics of corruption. The literature suggests that this topic has only been explored by a handful of well-respected international organisations and NGOs with specialized portfolios and offices within the region.

Box 5.1. Open Source Media Mapping: Corruption and illegal wildlife trade in the Focus countries

To conduct data collection on open source media incidents relating to corruption risks, the OECD collected over 300 unique reports over a period of time from 2008-2017. Information was recorded on the date and location of the alleged incident; the offence and species said to be involved; the type of corrupt actors said to be involved; the official and unofficial descriptions presented; the level of corruption said to be involved; and the status of the case.

Of the total reported cases, 17 were specific to the four countries of focus. Six occurred in Thailand, seven in Viet Nam, and three in Indonesia. Of the cases noted, four included to elephant ivory, four tiger, four rhino, four as "other" and one pangolin.

In the reported corruption events, over one third of all cases involved corruption among border and customs officials. Other corrupt actors within the reports included police, military, and government officials, notably forestry and environment officials. Of all the cases studied, the corruption related incidents were reported to be of an arrest, and no case involving a corruption related prosecution was found with the exception of a recent case in Viet Nam, the first arrest and prosecution of an officer for corruption offenses.

Source: OECD Research

Note: The open source media mapping exercise was undertaken with targeted word-string searches conducted in English, French and Spanish. Searches covered the word 'ivory' AND ('poaching' OR 'seizure' OR 'trial' OR 'fraud' OR 'accused' OR 'crime' OR 'arrested' OR 'guilty' OR 'jail' OR 'suspect' OR 'bribery' OR 'laundering' OR 'corrupt')5 . Over 300 cases were reviewed from 2008-2017, on a global scale.

Institutional Responses to Corruption

Public Awareness and engagement of civil society against corruption

Despite important improvements in economic conditions in Thailand, Viet Nam and Indonesia, economic development is still weighed down by from high rates of corruption. In a recent governance review of Southeast Asia, the OECD notes that "most SEA countries sit in the bottom half of 176 countries in Transparency International's Corruption Perceptions index" (OECD, 2019 (forthcoming)[9]).

Figure 5.1. Perception of Government Corruption, 2007 and 2017

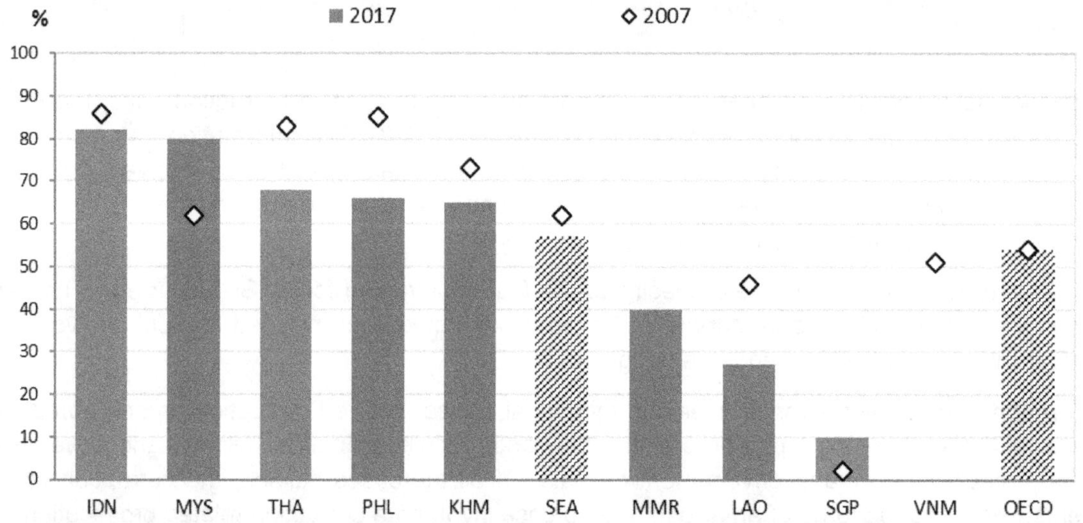

Note: Data correspond to the percentage of "Yes" answers to the question: "Is corruption widespread throughout the government in this country, or not?" Data for Malaysia are for 2015 rather than 2017. Data for Lao PDR are for 2008 rather than 2007. Data for Myanmar and Viet Nam are not included in the SEA average due to missing time series.
Source: OECD Governance at a Glance Southeast Asia 2018
doi.org/10.1787/888933840266

To respond to the challenges arising from corruption, Thailand, Indonesia and Viet Nam have recently adopted a number of measures to reinforce core public-integrity frameworks (OECD/ADB, 2018[10]). Several high-profile corruption cases involving senior government officials in Thailand and Indonesia and Viet Nam have taken place in public, and the public is becoming more aware of the effects of graft and abuse of power due to extensive media coverage of high-profile cases (GA-3, 2018[11]) (ENV Viet Nam, 2018[12]). In the case of illegal wildlife trade, a number of publicized cases have been prosecuted, with several respondents noting that the widespread media attention and public condemnation during these cases can be cited as a potential reason for successful convictions under a watchful public eye (TRAFFIC, 2018[13]) (ENV Viet Nam, 2018[12]).

However, in comparison to the studies from source countries, there are relatively fewer non-governmental actors in the field of anti-corruption programming. Fewer NGOs and International Organisations have dedicated projects or resources to anti-corruption or corruption prevention programming for illegal wildlife trade, and this topic is still widely viewed as an out-of-bounds issue for NGOs involved in tackling the illegal wildlife trade.

Overview of Anti-Corruption Frameworks in Relation to illegal wildlife trade

Anti-corruption agencies are responsible for overseeing public sector activities, from the delivery of everyday services to public to procurement, to the development of standards and guidelines to ensure the effective prevention of corruption in law enforcement. The below section outlines the structures of several of these core public-integrity agencies and frameworks and what ties these agencies have to wildlife crime.

Table 5.3. National Anti-Corruption Frameworks and illegal wildlife trade

Select relevant indicators and institutions

	Indonesia	Thailand	Viet Nam	Singapore
Principal Anti-Corruption Body	**Corruption Eradication Commission (KPK)**	**National Anti-corruption Commission (NACC)**	**Auditor General's Office**	**Corrupt Practices Investigation Bureau (CPIB)**
Anti-Corruption Strategy Title	National Strategy on Corruption Prevention and Eradication, 2011-2025	National Anti-Corruption Strategy, 2018-2037	National Strategy for Prevention and Combating Corruption towards 2020	Singapore Anti-Corruption Strategy
Corruption Prevention Polices Lead	KPK	NACC	Government Inspectorate	CPIB
Investigating Authority	High Level: KPK Lower Level: police	High Level: NACC, Lower Level: PACC	Ministry of Public Security	CPIB
Prosecuting Authority	Attorney General's Office	Office of the Attorney General	Supreme Peoples' Procuracy	Attorney General's Chambers
UNCAC Ratification	2006	2011	2009	2005
Environmental Crime Corruption Strategy	YES	YES	NO	NO
IWT Corruption Strategy	NO	NO	NO	NO
Whistle-blower program	YES	NO*	YES	YES
Number of known corruption prosecutions for illegal wildlife trade (past 10 years)	0	4**	1	0

Note: * The NACC has a witness protection programme, but has not yet implemented a whistle-blower program. **Corruption prosecutions may not have included specific corruption related charges, and instead reflect illegal wildlife trade crimes for public officials.
Source: OECD Research and interviews

Indonesia

The Indonesian Government has recently ramped up anti-corruption efforts. The result has been net improvements in the perception of corruption among respondents to the Transparency International Surveys thanks to a number of recent high-level corruption prosecutions led by the Indonesia Corruption Eradication Commission (KPK). However, according to a previous report form the OECD, corruption in Indonesia's forestry industry is a major cause of deforestation and an important revenue strain; related losses are estimated at USD $1 billion in 2014 from forest fires and USD $4 billion per year from illegal logging (OECD, 2017[14]). The National Strategy of Corruption Prevention and Eradication sets multi-agency, multi-year long term planning and objectives for enhancing public sector integrity. The agency in charge of implementing and leading the anti-corruption strategy (both prevention and high-level investigation) is the KPK. Other administrations involved in the Strategy include Indonesia National Police, Indonesia Financial Transaction Reports Analysis Center (PPATK), and the Attorney General's Office Special Crimes Unit.

The KPK operates an environmental crime task force on logging (Indonesia KPK, 2018[15]) (Indonesia AGO, 2018[16]) but there are no specific departments within the KPK that are known to address illegal wildlife trade. The KPK has a strict set of rules that at least two out of the following three conditions must be met to qualify for a Commission investigation and prosecutions. The crime in question must:

- Involve graft in excess of $US 63,000
- Involve a high level official
- Involve a crime of serious public concern

If the case in question does not meet the conditions noted above, the Indonesia National Police becomes the *de facto* charging and investigating authority. Based on the information gathered in this report, the KPK or the INP have to-date not charged any individuals with corruption crimes related to illegal wildlife trade (see box below).

Box 5.2. Illegal wildlife trade and the Indonesia Anti-Corruption Commission

During field interviews and research, the OECD found that no illegal wildlife trade cases have to-date been investigated by Indonesia's anti-corruption bureau, the KPK. According to KPK's requirements, corruption related to illegal wildlife trade crimes to-date have not met at least two out of the three following requirements: that the crimes in question must total over USD $63,000; that it must involve high level officials; or that it must be of great public concern (Indonesia KPK, 2018[15]). It is also reported that anti-corruption administrations lack the adequate staffing levels to conduct investigations for the majority of tip-offs and therefore there is a tendency for the administrations to focus only on less complex cases that are well known and have a clear outcome (such as forestry crimes instead of illegal wildlife trade) (TI, 2017[17]). This finding highlights the broader issue that the perception of illegal wildlife trade remains that of a low-revenue loss and relatively less serious form of corruption.

Thailand

Across Thailand, the overall perception of corruption has improved. Only 14% of respondents to a Global Barometer Survey thought that corruption had increased over the past year, the lowest figure in the region. Of the respondents to the survey, 72% believe that the government is doing well in tackling corruption (OECD, 2018[18]). Nevertheless, corruption remains an important challenge in sensitive sectors, notably among police and in public-facing service delivery: close to 80% of respondents, believe the police to be highly corrupt. Thailand has developed a National Strategic Plan for corruption. A number of agencies are in charge of the anti-corruption mandate in Thailand, with the Thailand National Anti-Corruption Commission (NACC) and the Public Sector Anti-Corruption Commission (PACC) responsible for prevention and investigation of corruption crimes. The Attorney General's Office (AG) is responsible for prosecuting corruption crimes. To-date the NACC has taken the lead in investigating and prosecuting wildlife crimes (and other environmental crimes).

In December 2019, Thailand's anti-corruption agency consolidated several divisions responsible for natural resources across the Commission into the NACC Bureau of Natural Resources and Environmental Corruption Inquiry (NACC, 2019[19]). This consolidation and creation of a larger Bureau focusing on environmental crimes has centralized a range of expertise to focus exclusively on environmental crimes. Specialized anti-corruption officers are now actively developing cases with a targeted approach to natural resources corruption. Natural resource cases may relate to wild fauna or flora, minerals and mining, forestry, fisheries, marine and coastline perseveration, and environmental degradation.

Since 2011, The NACC investigated and prosecuted four cases of corruption offenses and arrests related to illegal wildlife trade. These four cases have involved a range of public sector employees, with several cases involving high-level civil servants (Thailand NACC, 2018[20]). The recent consolidation of the NACC highlights the changing appreciation for corruption related to wildlife crime as a serious offense, and reflects the intention of the NACC to increase its efforts to tackle all forms of environmental crimes. However, the NACC has not yet prepared a national strategy to specifically target corruption with risk indicators for environment or wildlife crime.

Viet Nam

According to a 2017 UN Development Program (UNDP) citizen survey, Viet Nam has seen a net improvement of perception that governments are doing more to improve on this issue, with recent high-level corruption cases that have gained attention from the media. (CECODES, VFF-CRT, RTA & UNDP, 2017[21]). Viet Nam's anti-corruption administrations are less centralized than others are. Several ministries have internal anti-corruption departments, but the Ministry of Public Security (MPS) and the Government Inspectorate are the two main bodies in charge of investigating corruption crimes and setting preventive policy, respectively.

The Inspectorate General's office does not have a specific set of guidelines to counter illegal wildlife trade; however, the Ministry of Public Security, the enforcement body in charge of crimes that include illegal wildlife trade as well as Corruption, has an environmental police department. A number of cases relating to corruption and logging have taken place, but there is no specific anti-corruption strategy aimed explicitly at illegal wildlife trade. However, in August, Vietnamese authorities prosecuted the first known case of corruption in relation to illegal wildlife trade (TRAFFIC, 2018[22]).

Singapore

Singapore stands somewhat apart from the rest of the countries in this study, as it is presently ranked as the sixth least corrupt country in the world (TI, 2018[23]). Throughout the study among the focus countries, the OECD did not find evidence of any cases of corruption in relation to illegal wildlife trade.

Corruption risks at national borders

"Organized crime groups typically employ the tactics of collusion, corruption and protection to subvert the effectiveness of government regulators and law enforcers at important trade crossings" (UNODC, 2013[24]). Existing laws prohibit the import of CITES products, but often legal loopholes and gaps enable the open trading of several forms of illegal wildlife trade products within the domestic economy. As a result, national borders can become a first and last line of defence against illegal wildlife trade within a given country. Throughout the interviews conducted in this study, the OECD's findings pointed to high corruption risks at national points of entry. The following section offers a detailed description of how and where corruption risks are most pronounced in the countries studied. As previously noted within this chapter, several of the cases relate to findings from Indonesia, Viet Nam and Thailand, however no cases involving corruption and illegal wildlife trade have been reported for Singapore.

Corruption risks for Customs

Customs officials play a central role in the facilitation of global trade and the assurance that goods cross borders in a safe, effective and rapid manner. Customs officials are responsible for the collection of revenue, as well as the enforcement of various laws and regulations that are vital to ensuring the safety and security of citizens. Complex customs procedures, gaps in predictability and accountability, low rates of morale or perceived low remuneration and inadequate recruiting diligence can present certain risks for corruption for customs officials (OECD, 2017[25]). Such risk factors, combined with significant discretionary powers of customs officials posted at the border can lead to an abuse of power (U4, 2018[26]). Gaps in integrity among customs can expose societies to global threats engendered by illicit trade. High rates of reported corruption in have been tied to illicit activities, such as bribery for expedited processing; tax evasion; fraud; and smuggling of counterfeits, narcotics, and numerous other forms of illicit trade (OECD, 2017[25]). The 2018 OECD report on illegal wildlife trade and Corruption in Southern and Eastern Africa finds that the export and transit of illegal wildlife trade benefits from networks of corruption among customs officials (OECD, 2018[8]). Throughout the below sections, empirical evidence found during OECD interviews points to the risk of corruption facing customs officials at border crossings in Southeast Asia.

Corruption at Airports

Major airports in Southeast Asia are significant hubs for illegal wildlife trade. The Air-mode (which is composed of passenger and commercial air-cargo), is commonly used for high-value products such as rhino horn or relatively small quantities of ivory, and live animal trade (C4ADS, 2018[27]) (Indonesia Customs, 2018[28]). According to recent reports, the number of rhino horns seized at airports from 2016 to 2017 has also increased by 300% (C4ADS, 2018[27]).

Airports involve a range of government and private sector stakeholders, each with their own set of responsibilities and risk factors. Airport security must screen bags and air cargo primarily for safety and security reasons, whereas customs officials conduct screenings for prohibited items and controlled goods[6]. Behind the scenes, baggage and cargo handlers, airport officials and airline staff operate within secured areas, and have privileged access to customs controlled areas or secure perimeters. Each of the stakeholders mentioned is at risk of corruption from illegal wildlife trade traffickers.

In airports, customs administrations face significant pressure from corruption risks, notably bribery due to their position as the last line of defence against foreign illicit commodities. Respondents familiar with investigations into wildlife crime in several countries noted that customs officers have been known to accept bribes to avoid inspections (FD-1, 2018[29]) (Thailand NACC, 2018[20]).

Box 5.3. KPK Audit of Corruption Risks from Customs in Indonesia:

In 2014, the KPK undertook an undercover audit and review of the integrity systems in place at major airports. The findings, detailed below, indicate the level of risk and the institutional gaps that are present at major airports in the region. These results highlight the level of vulnerability of customs officials to bribery and corruption schemes.

The 2014 review found that a number of officials at the airport posed an important corruption risk and above all, the customs officials were at the highest risk of corruption. While this study was not focused on any specific form of smuggling, the KPK report raised the alarm to the fact that customs officials remained open to bribery and in some cases extorted money during the undercover audit of their integrity and performance.

Officials from KPK did not pursue any cases due to the threshold pre-requisites for severity of crimes not met. The KPK passed along the audit findings the Indonesia National Police for further investigation; however, no arrests or investigations are known to have taken place for the violations of integrity standards that were documented in this review (Indonesia KPK, 2018[15]).

From the findings of the KPK report, authors noted, “bribery, gratification and extortion often occur in the import services because of a lack of oversight, and low integrity of officials” (Indonesia KPK, 2018[15]). The following recommendations are proposed by the anti-corruption administration to enhance resilience to corruption at airports:

- Assess the regulations and procedures on import and export.
- Harmonize import and export licensing systems
- Enhance the integrity of customs with a code of ethics, and strengthen the institutions
- Unannounced inspections in ports can help to enhance security, particularly for high-risk commodities.

These recommendations highlight some of proposed ideas that are touted by anti-corruption administrations as part of part of a broader integrity toolkit against all forms of illicit activity at border crossings. However, gaps between recommendation and implementation are common. Investigations into customs corruption are also infrequent due to resource constraints and competing political priorities among anti-corruption administrations (Indonesia KPK, 2018[15]) (Thailand NACC, 2018[20]).

Aside from Customs, other public authorities can also pose important risks for corrupt practises to facilitate illegal wildlife trade. For example, in one case in Indonesia, a government official working for airport security was arrested over a smuggling operation for the export of live reptiles and snakes out of the country and into Japan. The official in question was sentenced with aiding and abetting a crime (but was not sentenced through corruption courts) (Indonesia National Police, 2018[30]). Senior government officials have also been caught smuggling or facilitating the entrance of illegal wildlife trade products. In Thailand, government officials were apprehended facilitating the entry of two travellers out of the customs controlled arrivals area:

Box 5.4. Corruption as a key facilitator of Wildlife Crime at Bangkok Suvarnabhumi International Airport

In 2017, several cases involving corruption and illegal wildlife trade took place at Thailand's major international airport. Below are some of the major interdictions of illegal wildlife trade facilitated by wildlife crime:

In March 2017, Royal Thai Customs officials seized over 20 rhino horns in the country's major airport. Two civilian travellers arriving from Viet Nam and Thailand (respectively) arrived at the same time as a flight from Ethiopia, and proceeded to pick up two unclaimed suitcases from this luggage arrivals belt. Two police officers and a senior ministry of justice official then met the travellers, who attempted to escort them and their new suitcases through customs inspections.

When questioned by Customs, the senior Thai official insisted that the bags contained wine and that they should not be inspected. Once stopped the official and subsequently attempted to bribe customs officials.

In 2018, the two travellers and ministry of justice official were sentenced each to four years in jail for smuggling and tax evasion. However, no corruption related laws were used to prosecute the official in question.

Source: OECD research and Interviews

The case above involves the transit of goods across at least three countries (as rhinos are not native in Ethiopia); the arrival of unaccompanied air-traveller baggage from an international airport; co-ordinated flight arrivals from three separate countries; and agents from two distinct government administrations, suggests a high degree of co-ordination from a transnational criminal syndicate involved in illegal wildlife trade and corruption. However, despite the level of complexity and corrupt acts involved, the officials (including the senior ministry of justice official) were not charged with corruption related offenses.

Employees from the private sector in positions of trust can also be a threat to integrity and security of the global trade chain. During interviews with customs officials at one of the major airports in Southeast Asia, the OECD learned that internal conspiracies involving transnational criminal networks and private actors are also a known corruption risk. Recent seizures of rhino horn at one of the region's largest airports illustrates the level of complexity of these operations:

Box 5.5. Internal Conspiracies at Major International Airports: Private Sector Actors and Corruption

In 2017, customs at a major international airport, officials seized a shipment of rhino horns on a domestic arrivals baggage claim. Upon investigation, officials learned that the bag had actually arrived from an international destination in Africa, but the baggage tag had been swapped to allow it to arrive into domestic arrivals (which do not require customs clearance).

Officials determined that the baggage tag on the goods seized was likely to have been swapped after arrival, indicating that an internal conspiracy was in play. The seizures of such bags in several instances suggests that there are well-coordinated efforts from transnational criminals who have used their security access to commit smuggling offenses. The modus operandi involving baggage-tag printing or switching requires communication among transnational networks that are well established. This approach may also be used for other forms of illicit trade, suggesting that criminal syndicates employ these abuses of power for a wider range of crimes.

Source: OECD Research and interviews

Several experts and officials interviewed noted that airport staff represent an important corruption risk at airports, because they have extensive knowledge of the security practises and gaps that can be exploited for all forms of illicit products, including narcotics, and other goods. The above case suggests that private companies that are operating at airports are at risk of being infiltrated by organized crime. However, there was no indication that the corruption reached beyond the level of individuals. Customs officials noted that once uncovered, ground-staff operating companies and airport authorities are co-operative and assist with the investigation.

Corruption at Land Border Crossings:

OECD interviews undertaken with relevant experts and officials revealed that land borders are vulnerable points for corruption risks, with customs officials who are most often cited as being susceptible to corruption such as bribery (Nam, 2016[31]) (NG-1, 2018[32]) (IO-1, 2018[33]) (GA-2, 2018[34]) (Indonesia KPK, 2018[15]). The discussions relating to border crossings focused on Thailand and Viet Nam in connection to Myanmar, Laos PDR, Malaysia, Cambodia and China. Particular focus is given to the Thai-Myanmar border and the Viet Nam-Laos and Viet Nam-China borders[7].

Several respondents noted that that there is a significant amount of trafficking along the northern international border crossings between China and Viet Nam and in the southern region between Viet Nam and Laos, as well as Cambodia[8]. Seizures of pangolin are reported to be the most traded form of illegal wildlife trade along the border regions of focus, followed by other goods such as carved ivory, big cats, rhino horn and various live animals (UNODC, 2013[35]). The role of the northern border regions highlights Viet Nam's position as a major transit and transhipment country for illegal wildlife trade along the route to China. The below case study on Mong Cai Border city in Viet Nam also highlights the role of corruption in facilitating the illegal wildlife trade into its final destination market.

The transit and export of illegal wildlife trade products concerns all forms of illegal wildlife trade, both domestic and foreign-sourced products. Land borders are the most important points in the cross-border illegal big-cat trade, as these CITES species are smuggled across borders without certification. The trade is conducted in most cases with "impunity, despite international laws to prohibit the trade in these species" (TRAFFIC, 2010[36]). In some neighbouring countries such as Myanmar or Laos, it was reported that there are open markets that benefit from special arrangements through corrupt state officials. In particular, certain free trade zones (FTZs) in neighbouring countries are hotspots for illegal wildlife trade.

Box 5.6. Corruption, Money Laundering and Illegal Wildlife Trade in Free Trade Zones

Previous work undertaken by the OECD and EUIPO has highlighted the heightened risk from illicit trade in Free Trade Zones (FTZs) (OECD/EUIPO, 2018[37]). According to several interviewees, the gaps in transparency and legal ambiguities in FTZs are similarly exploited in several Southeast Asian countries and facilitate trafficking and processing of a wide variety of products including counterfeits, narcotics, alcohol, tobacco, pharmaceuticals, wildlife and humans. (Martin, 2017[38]) (NG-2, 2018[39]), (GA-3, 2018[11]) . Widespread corruption and illicit financial flows are recognized as the sustaining factor within these zones (U.S. DOT, 2018[40]).

Laotian FTZs along the tristate land border with Thailand and Myanmar are an example of how these zones are used to traffic in illegal wildlife trade. The Golden Triangle Special Economic Zone in Laos offers tourists a wide variety of illegal wildlife trade products, including live specimens and products from domestically sourced big cats and internationally trafficked pieces of ivory, elephant skin, rhino horn and a range of illegal wildlife trade products. According to the wildlife NGO Traffic:

> *Many of Asia's poached and farmed Tigers pass through the Golden Triangle, where they end up in tiger wine, on dinner tables, in dubious medicines or as luxury items and jewellery. The trade in live elephants, elephant skin, combined with continuing demand for ivory, is threatening elephant populations from Asia to Africa. Bear farms are rampant across the region, where both Sun Bears and Asiatic Black Bears—mostly captured in the wild—are kept in cages while their bile is collected for traditional medicine and folk remedies. (TRAFFIC, 2017[41])*

In one recent case announced by the United States Department of Treasury, a transnational criminal network based out of Hong Kong are said to be operating out of the Golden Triangle FTZ in Laos, and operates a nearby casino adjacent to the FTZ. Large sums of money are laundered through these zones, into and out of adjacent Thailand and onwards towards other countries. illegal wildlife trade is among a wide variety of illegal activities that include child prostitution, arms trafficking and drug smuggling reported in this zone by numerous sources (SCMP, 2018[42]) (U.S. DOT, 2018[40]) (Nuwer, 2018[43]). Given the widespread value of wildlife products in the region, it is likely that illegal wildlife trade products are one of the several conduits for proceeds of crime and money laundering.

Box 5.7. Corruption and Smuggling along the Viet Nam China Border

Mong Cai City is one of the largest known international crossings for illegal wildlife trade from Viet Nam into China. The city plays host to numerous border crossing points and there are a number of known illegal smuggling routes in the nearby region through the narrow Ka Long river crossings (EAL, 2017[44]) (NG-2, 2018[39]) (Reuters, 2015[45]). According to OECD interviews, there are several ways to get goods through border checks relying on corruption. One is to personally bribe or pay-off border officers, where a fee is given based on the value or quantity of the goods. Another system involves the use of a local "Kingpin" that arranges broader protection from regional officials at a higher level. The latter is used more often for larger shipments. According to reports from investigations, Kingpins offer prices based on the products and their quantity. For example, the cost of exporting pangolin scales varies from USD $10-15 per kg. Other "special goods" such as ivory or rhino horn depend on the current enforcement climate in neighbouring China. The so-called Kingpins are several in number, and are known to smuggle a wide variety of animal products, such as frozen goods, meats, seafood and agricultural products to evade taxes and commit fraud (Reuters, 2015[45]). In a recent case, Chinese authorities cracked down on a smuggling operation through Mong Cai that had imported sub-standard meat products intended for restaurants, with some pieces of meat dating back to the 1970s (SCMP, 2018[46]).

Highly professionalized organized criminal groups co-ordinate the smuggling of a wide variety of products in the border crossings, often each specializing in a sub-set of trafficked products (NG-2, 2018[39]). Traffickers are known to rely heavily on 'mules' or 'feet' in this border region as well (Reuters, 2015[45]). According to the head of provincial customs, "Most people involve[ed] in the smuggling cases are border residents or labourers who regularly cross the border" (Viet Nam News, 2018[47]). Residents in the border region have special identification cards that allow them and are not subject to controls for most verifications, and are exempt from duties and taxes up to approximately USD $89. A recent case involving seizure of ivory carried by a 13 year-old into China also illustrates how children are being used by organized criminals because of their "relatively lower likelihood of inspection" (NG-2, 2018[39]) (Khanh Lynh, 2018[48]). Thanks to the same gaps in institutional capacities and lapses in integrity, other risks including human trafficking, weapons smuggling and the drugs trade are also known to be a converging threat through these same border points.

Respondents in Viet Nam noted that many of the border crossings are not adequately staffed, and the relatively remote location of these crossings makes oversight of border officers' conduct particularly difficult (NG-1, 2018[32]). As a result, corruption or simple non-enforcement of laws is a commonly cited risk. Along the northern land border between Viet Nam and China, tourists are reportedly able to cross into the country to purchase ivory and rhino horns. To bring the goods home, tourists can themselves buy small pieces of carved ivory and transport them on their person across the border. Larger shipments can be co-ordinated through brokers who are familiar with smuggling methods and bribery of customs officials (NG-1, 2018[32]) (EAL, 2017[44]).

Thailand's land border also plays an important role in the illegal wildlife trade chain. The international crossings between Thailand and Myanmar and between Laos PDR and Thailand are important risk-areas for the illegal trade in native species, such as bear bile and tiger parts and local fauna and flora. According to a recent study, border towns play host to a number of open markets that sell illegal wildlife trade products openly (Min, 2018[49]). For example, the Sai-Tachilek border crossing in Chiang Rai Province is part of a border market in Myanmar that sells all forms of illegal wildlife trade products to tourists, including Thai and Chinese tourists and middlemen (Oswell, 2010[50]).

Corruption at Ports and Seaports

In this report, the OECD has not studied the linkages between corruption at seaports and the illegal wildlife trade. However, the risk profile and the evidence of corruption writ-large at ports in Viet Nam, Thailand and Indonesia suggest that officials in positions of power are either opportunistically leveraging corruption or are doing so in a co-ordinated manner to facilitate the entrance of a much wide range of goods into the country. For example, in April 2018, a Vietnamese Customs Officer in a shipping port and Export Processing Zone outside of Ho Chi Minh City was sentenced to 12 years in jail for accepting bribes and abuse of power to facilitate trafficking and trade fraud. Court reporting indicates that the individual in question was also likely acting as part of a broader network (Hai Duyen, 2018[51]). In 2017, the Viet Nam Ministry of Public Security arrested two customs officers on corruption charges 2017 over the disappearance of over 200 shipping containers as part of a co-ordinated scheme to import goods in-transit (Quoc Thang, 2017[52]). In 2016, Indonesia National Police arrested a customs official at the Java Province's largest port for taking bribes in exchange for facilitating entry of goods into the country (Jakarta Post, 2016[53]).

Several seizures of large, multi-tonne shipments of illegal wildlife trade have taken place at marine ports of entry into Indonesia, Thailand, Singapore and Viet Nam. For example, between 2016 and 2017, Viet Nam customs seized over 7 tonnes of ivory from a single co-ordinated organisation using the same smuggling methods (Viet Nam Customs, 2017[54]). The ability to move several large, multi-tonne high value and high volume products into seaports indicates a high level of sophistication.

Anti-Corruption efforts for other Environmental Crimes

As highlighted throughout this chapter, there are few cases of corruption investigations and prosecutions in relation to illegal wildlife trade among the focus countries. Just five cases have been confirmed in only two of the focus countries (Thailand and Viet Nam). In Indonesia, where corruption represents a known risk to illegal wildlife trade, there have been no instances of successful prosecutions of officials complicit in the facilitation of wildlife crimes. However, anti-corruption officials have successfully prosecuted a range of other environmental crimes. The section below highlights several cases where corruption cases have taken place for other environmental crimes, and suggest that there are avenues for further engagement and inclusion of more environmental crimes (such as illegal wildlife trade) into anti-corruption efforts.

Corruption and logging crimes in Indonesia:

The Indonesia Ministry of Environment and Forestry is responsible for several areas of enforcement for wildlife crime, including forest fires (for clearing and burning); encroachment; illegal logging; wildlife crime and pollution or toxic waste dumping. All of these offenses can be facilitated by corruption. Of the wider range of crimes that fall under the responsibility of wildlife enforcement agencies, illegal logging was raised as a particularly common form of environmental crime for which corruption has been identified as a key facilitator. Indonesia's anti-corruption commission, the KPK estimates the losses from logging to total some USD $9 billion in state revenues from timber sales between 2003 and 2014 (TI, 2017[17]). Many of the losses incurred from illicit trade in timber is due to the corruption of government officials who directly benefit from sales or through licensing concessions (Indonesia KPK, 2018[15]) (Indonesia MEF, 2018[55]).

Indonesian government has taken a number of steps to tackle illegal logging. A presidential decree was issued for the creation of a National Task Force on Logging and agencies have used a multi-agency approach to illegal logging. This multi-agency task force involves direct and pro-active co-ordination between the Ministry of Environment and Forestry; Customs; National Police; Quarantine; the Anticorruption Commission (KPK); the Indonesia Financial Transaction Reports Analysis Center (PPATK); and the Office of the Attorney General (OAG).

The results from the multi-agency approach in logging crimes has translated into a series of successful high-level prosecutions related to corruption (and money laundering). In 2014, the former governor of Riau Province was sentenced to 14 years in jail and USD $90,000 in fines for embezzlement which stemmed from illegally issuing logging permits (Mongabay, 2014[56]).

Conclusion

Complex networks of criminal syndicates employ the services of corrupt officials to ensure that the poaching, import, export, sale and transit of illegal wildlife products. However, the current body of evidence proving definitive proof of the linkages between corruption and illegal wildlife trade remains small: research by the OECD has found just five cases of charges or prosecutions of individuals for corruption related to wildlife crime in just two countries.

In support of advancing this research, the OECD's interviews have highlighted a significant range of corruption risks along supply chains with a focus of this chapter on the use of national points of entry for corruption. At ports, airports and road crossings, actors vulnerable to corruption at border (namely police, customs, and other actors in the private sector) offer their services in exchange for profits or personal gain. The risks of corruption at ports and airports are heightened by the fact that illegal wildlife trade products are often relatively easy to "launder" once in the countries in question. Transnational criminal syndicates are likely to dedicate even greater effort (and resource) to ensuring that illegal wildlife trade products move through these choke points, thus adding further pressure on law enforcement officials at national points of entry. Furthermore, illegal wildlife trade along border crossings relies on a similar modus operandi to illicit trade in other products. Any illegal crossing of illegal wildlife trade using corrupt means is a likely signal of that other forms of illicit trade (such as narcotics, counterfeits and others) are making their way through these same border crossings.

Throughout the research, the researchers took note of a number of other corruption risks mentioned, notably in courts, evidence rooms and stockpiles, and among licensing officials. The anecdotal evidence collected on these topics suggests that additional in-depth and targeted research and data collection on a wide range of corruption risks is necessary to explore the dynamics and modus operandi for corruption in relation to illegal wildlife trade.

References

AU (2015), *African Strategy on Combating Illegal Exploitation and Illegal Trade in Wild Fauna and Flora in Africa Stratégie Africaine sur la lutte contre l'Exploitation Illégale et le Commerce Illicite de la Faune et de la Flore Sauvages en Afrique*, https://wedocs.unep.org/bitstream/handle/20.500.11822/20825/African%20Strategy%20Strategy%20Africaine%20AU.pdf?sequence=1&%3BisAllowed= (accessed on 29 April 2019). [3]

C4ADS (2018), *In Plane Sight: Wildlife Trafficking in the Air Transport Sector*, http://www.routespartnership.org (accessed on 8 November 2018). [27]

CECODES, VFF-CRT, RTA & UNDP (2017), *The 2017 Viet Nam Governance and Public Administration PerformanceIndex (PAPI 2017): Measuring Citizens' Experiences*, A Joint Policy Research Paper by the Centre for Community Support andDevelopment Studies (CECODES), Centre for Research and Training of the Viet Nam Fatherland Front (VFF-CRT), Real-Time Analytics, and United Nations Development Programme (UNDP), http://papi.org.vn/eng/wp-content/uploads/2018/04/2017PAPI_Report_ENG.pdf. [21]

EAL (2017), *Grinding Rhino: Operatin Red Cloud Investigative Report*. [44]

ENV Viet Nam (2018), *Interview with Education for Nature (ENV), Hanoi, Vietnam, August 20, 2018.* [12]

EU (2016), "EU Action Plan against Wildlife Trafficking (COM(2016) 87 final) Environment", http://dx.doi.org/10.2779/016138. [4]

FD-1 (2018), *Interview with Foreign Delegation 1, August 21, 2018.* [29]

G20 (2017), *Annex to G20 Leaders Declaration: G20 High Level Principles on Combatting Corruption Related to Illegal Trade in Wildlife and Wildlife Products*, https://www.consilium.europa.eu/media/23552/2017-g20-acwg-wildlife-en.pdf (accessed on 22 January 2018). [5]

GA-2 (2018), *Interview with Government Agency 2, August 21, 2018.* [34]

GA-3 (2018), *Interview with Government Agency 3, Bangkok, Thailand, August 23, 2018.* [11]

Hai Duyen (2018), *Corrupt customs officer gets 12 years behind bars in Ho Chi Minh City*, VN Express News, https://e.vnexpress.net/news/news/corrupt-customs-officer-gets-12-years-behind-bars-in-ho-chi-minh-city-3735207.html (accessed on 7 December 2018). [51]

Indonesia AGO (2018), *In person interview at the Office of the Attorney General: Special Task Force on Natural Resources,October 18, 2018.* [16]

Indonesia Customs (2018), *Interview with the Directorate General of Customs, Ministry of Finance, October 18, 2018.* [28]

Indonesia KPK (2018), *Interview with Indonesia Corruption Eradication Commission (KPK), October 19, 218.* [15]

Indonesia MEF (2018), *Interview with Indonesia Directorate General for Law Enforcement, Ministry of Environment and Forestry, October 17, 2018.* [55]

Indonesia National Police (2018), *Interview with Indonesia National Police, Special Directorate, Illegal Wildlife Trade, October 19, 2018.* [30]

IO-1 (2018), *Interview with Inter-Governmental Organisation 1, August 20, 2018.* [33]

Jakarta Post (2016), *Customs official of Semarang port arrested in illegal levy case*, https://www.thejakartapost.com/news/2016/11/11/customs-official-of-semarang-port-arrested-in-illegal-levy-case-1478841132.html (accessed on 18 January 2019). [53]

Khanh Lynh (2018), *Vietnam investigating China's detention of Vietnamese girl for ivory smuggling*, VN Express News, https://e.vnexpress.net/news/news/vietnam-investigating-china-s-detention-of-vietnamese-girl-for-ivory-smuggling-3751148.html (accessed on 7 December 2018). [48]

Martin, E. (2017), *Interview with Esmond Bradley Martin.* [38]

Min, S. (2018), *A Final Report on Investigation of Wildlife Trade in Myanmar-Thailand Border Cities under Growing Trans-boundary Economic Trade*, https://www.rufford.org/files/19203-2%20Detailed%20Final%20Report.pdf (accessed on 7 December 2018). [49]

Mongabay (2014), *Indonesia politician gets 14 years in jail for illegal permits, forest corruption*, Mongabay News, https://news.mongabay.com/2014/03/indonesia-politician-gets-14-years-in-jail-for-illegal-permits-forest-corruption/ (accessed on 11 December 2018). [56]

NACC (2019), *Information Received from NACC During follow-up conversations, March 2019.* [19]

Nam, E. (2016), *The Penal Code Revision: A wildlife protection milestone for Vietnam*, http://www.envietnam.or (accessed on 27 November 2018). [31]

NG-1 (2018), *Interview with Non-Government Organisation 1, Vietnam, August 20, 2018.* [32]

NG-2 (2018), *Interview with Non-governmental organisation 2, Indonesia, October 17, 2018.* [39]

Nuwer, R. (2018), *Poached*, De Capo Press. [43]

OECD (2018), *OECD Integrity Review of Thailand: Towards Coherent and Effective Integrity Policies*, OECD Public Governance Reviews, OECD Publishing, Paris, https://dx.doi.org/10.1787/9789264291928-en. [18]

OECD (2018), *Strengthening Governance and Reducing Corruption Risks to Tackle Illegal Wildlife Trade: Lessons from East and Southern Africa*, Illicit Trade, OECD Publishing, Paris, https://dx.doi.org/10.1787/9789264306509-en. [8]

OECD (2017), *Indonesia Policy Brief: Bribery and Corruption*, http://www.oecd.org/policy-briefs (accessed on 20 November 2018). [14]

OECD (2017), *Integrity in Customs: Taking Stock of Good Practises*, OECD Publishing, Paris, http://www.oecd.org/corruption/ethics/G20-integrity-in-customs-taking-stock-of-good-practices.pdf (accessed on 11 December 2018). [25]

OECD (2019 (forthcoming)), *Government at a Glance Southeast Asia 2019*, http://www.oecd.org/publications/government-at-a-glance-southeast-asia-2018-9789264305915-en.htm (accessed on 29 April 2019). [9]

OECD/ADB (2018), *Government at a Glance: Southeast Asia 2018*, OECD Publishing, Paris, http://dx.doi.org/doi.org/10.1787/888933840266. [10]

OECD/EUIPO (2018), *Trade in Counterfeit Goods and Free Trade Zones: Evidence from Recent Trends*, OECD Publishing, Paris/EUIPO, https://dx.doi.org/10.1787/9789264289550-en. [37]

Oswell, A. (2010), *THE BIG CAT TRADE IN MYANMAR AND THAILAND A TRAFFIC SOUTHEAST ASIA REPORT*, TRAFFIC Southeast Asia, http://assets.wwf.es/downloads/traffic_species_mammals61_1_.pdf (accessed on 8 November 2018). [50]

Quoc Thang (2017), *Customs officer arrested after 213 containers disappear from Saigon port*, VNExpress, https://e.vnexpress.net/news/news/customs-officer-arrested-after-213-containers-disappear-from-saigon-port-3639644.html (accessed on 18 January 2019). [52]

Reuters (2015), *China meat smuggling crackdown stokes risky underground trade*, Reuters, https://www.reuters.com/article/china-smuggling-meat-idUSL4N0ZF34020150715 (accessed on 10 December 2018). [45]

SCMP (2018), *A Mr Big of wildlife trafficking: could elusive Laos casino operator be behind rackets that run to drugs, child prostitution?*, South China Morning Post, https://www.scmp.com/magazines/post-magazine/long-reads/article/2141464/mr-big-wildlife-trafficking-could-elusive-laos (accessed on 10 December 2018). [42]

SCMP (2018), *'Illegal smuggling routes' exposed after rotting meat from the 1970s seized by Chinese customs*, South China Morning Post, https://www.scmp.com/news/china/society/article/1825584/smugglers-also-shipping-frozen-beef-china-through-india-and (accessed on 10 December 2018). [46]

Thailand NACC (2018), *Interview with Thailand National Anti-corruption Commission, July 5, 2018.* [20]

TI (2018), *Corruption Perception Index*, https://www.transparency.org/whoweare/contact/org/nc_indonesia/2. [23]

TI (2017), *Tackling Corruption to Protect the World's Forests: How the Eu can Rise to the Challenge*, Transparency International, https://transparency.eu/wp-content/uploads/2017/01/TI-GW-Anti-corruption-briefing-January-2017.pdf (accessed on 11 December 2018). [17]

TRAFFIC (2018), *Former Hanoi Customs officer gets 16-years following ivory and rhino horn theft from government warehouse*, https://www.traffic.org/news/former-hanoi-customs-officer-gets-16-years/ (accessed on 3 December 2018). [22]

TRAFFIC (2018), *Interview with TRAFFIC, Bangkok, Thailand, July 15, 2018.* [13]

TRAFFIC (2017), *Golden Triangle under spotlight as illegal wildlife trade hub*, https://www.traffic.org/news/golden-triangle-under-spotlight-as-illegal-wildlife-trade-hub/ (accessed on 10 December 2018). [41]

TRAFFIC (2010), *The Big Cat Trade in Myanmar and Thailand*, https://www.cdt.ch/files/docs/5875b90a73644945622fc204eeef0dd9.pdf. [36]

U.S. DOT (2018), *Treasury Sanctions the Zhao Wei Transnational Criminal Organization*, https://home.treasury.gov/news/press-releases/sm0272 (accessed on 10 December 2018). [40]

U4 (2018), "Combatting corruption in tax and customs administration in AsiaPacific", https://www.u4.no/publications/combatting-corruption-in-tax-and-customs-administration-in-asia-pacific.pdf (accessed on 7 December 2018). [26]

UN (2017), *Resolution of the General Assembly: Tackling illicit trafficking in wildlife A/71/L.88 - E - A/71/L.88*, https://undocs.org/A/71/L.88 (accessed on 29 April 2019). [1]

UN (2015), *UN Genergal Assembly Resolution Tackling illicit trafficking in wildlifeA/69/L.80 - E - A/69/L.80*, https://undocs.org/A/69/L.80 (accessed on 25 April 2019). [2]

UNODC (2015), *Wildlife and Forest Crime Analytic Toolkit: Vietnam.* [6]

UNODC (2013), *Border Control in the Greater Mekong Sub-region*, https://www.unodc.org/documents/southeastasiaandpacific/2014/01/patrol/Border_Control_GMS_report.pdf (accessed on 7 December 2018). [35]

UNODC (2013), “Transnational Organized Crime in East Asia and the Pacific A Threat Assessment”, http://www.unodc.org/res/cld/bibliography/transnational-organized-crime-in-east-asia-and-the-pacific-a-threat-assessment_html/TOCTA_EAP_web.pdf (accessed on 9 November 2018). [24]

Viet Nam Customs (2017), *Why are ivory smuggling suspended?*, Customs News, https://customsnews.vn/why-are-ivory-smuggling-suspended-5254.html (accessed on 7 December 2018). [54]

Viet Nam News (2018), *Border residents join smuggling foreign currency and goods*, Vietnam News, https://vietnamnews.vn/society/451600/border-residents-join-smuggling-foreign-currency-and-goods.html#uPlCV8AzAUURBzcm.97 (accessed on 7 December 2018). [47]

WWF/TRAFFIC (2015), *Working Together To Combat Illegal And Unsustainable Wildlife Trade Corruption In Wildlife Conservation: A Primer Strategies For Fighting*, http://www.traffic.org (accessed on 29 April 2019). [7]

Notes

[1] For clarity and consistency, the OECD uses the Transparency international definition of ‘corruption’ as the ‘abuse of entrusted power for private gain’. This definition was also referenced in the 2018 publication of the OECD on Corruption and IWT in Southern and Eastern Africa.

[2] Corruption is found to be an enabler of IWT in all focus countries, with the exception of Singapore.

[3] Direct assistance may be the provision of arms and equipment for poachers, as well as the direct participation in the killing and taking of protected animals.

[4] Passive assistance may include sharing of locations of animals or patrols, provisions of expertise and knowledge or non-enforcement of laws in exchange for bribes in the event of apprehension.

[5] CITES officials have been reported to be assisting IWT products to gain entry through criminal conspiracies at airports.

[6] However, if a security official spots a suspicious package for other non-security related reasons; they may also refer these to customs who have authority to intervene at any point to enforce relevant laws on exports and imports.

[7] It is also widely documented that land borders between Malaysia and Indonesia are also implicated in illicit trade and corruption but for the purposes of this report, this issue was not explored.

[8] While it is known that significant illicit trade along the land borders between Malaysia and Indonesia takes place, the OECD found no information referencing specific issues related to corruption in this region. Further research is needed to conduct an assessment of the corruption risks in this border region.

6 Proceeds of Crime, Illicit Financial Flows and Money Laundering

This chapter examines responses of national enforcement agencies and the international community to tackle illicit financial flows associated with the illegal wildlife trade. The findings indicate that most of the focus countries have not reportedly used anti-money laundering provisions or "follow the money" approaches to tackle the illegal wildlife trade. Financial investigations are an exceptional occurrence. Greater strategic planning and engagement with anti-money laundering authorities is necessary to determine if money laundering investigations are useful and what further planning, programming, resourcing and co-ordination is needed to ensure successful investigations and prosecutions of money laundering for wildlife crime.

Introduction

Profit is the most important driver behind the global illegal wildlife trade. The sale of illegal wildlife products generates billions in revenue annually (Nellemann; et al, 2016[160]). Meanwhile, the illicit financial flows from illegal wildlife trade transit around the globe through the global financial system and into the hands of criminal networks. Along the way, the proceeds of crime run afoul of laws and international conventions, weaken institutions by fuelling more poaching expeditions and reward corruption. Proceeds of crime are integrated into the legitimate financial system through Money Laundering, the process of concealing illicit gains that were generated from criminal activity (OECD, 2019[161]).

Financial Intelligence Units (FIUs) and police can conduct, or provide support to parallel investigations of financial crimes addressing proceeds of crime and money laundering. These investigations can be useful in targeting a wider network of actors and increasing institutional capacities against wildlife crimes (FATF, 2012[162]). Despite this, evidence suggests that "follow the money" approaches, notably the involvement of FIUs, remain scarce for wildlife crimes in nearly all countries (OECD, 2018[49]) (UNODC/APG, 2017[163]) (Haenlein and Keatinge, 2017[164]). Indeed, across the four focus countries, the OECD has found that just one has successfully employed a financial investigation in only two instances.

Without asset seizure, forfeiture and penalties for money laundering, wildlife crime remains a "low-risk, high-reward" form of criminality (OECD, 2016[9]). This chapter identifies what factors have prevented the widespread use of money laundering laws to prosecute illegal wildlife trade in Southeast Asia and what further measures may be needed to integrate financial investigations into the broader efforts to tackle illegal wildlife trade.

Overview of Frameworks to Combat Money Laundering

International Standards on Combatting Money Laundering

The International Standards on Combatting Money Laundering are set by the Financial Action Task Force (FATF) Recommendations, which "set standards [and] promote effective implementation of legal, regulatory and operational measures for combating money laundering, terrorist financing and the financing of proliferation, and other related threats to the integrity of the international financial system (FATF, 2012[162])." The Asia Pacific Group on Money Laundering (APG) is the FATF Style Regional Body (FSRB) co-ordinating implementation of the FATF standards in the region (FATF, 2019[165]). The APG is composed of over 41 member jurisdictions and several other observer countries, including all ASEAN members. The APG and FATF co-ordinate to conduct mutual evaluation reviews (MERs) to measure technical compliance and effectiveness of national and international policies against money laundering (FATF, 2019[166]). In addition to assessing technical compliance and effectiveness of existing money laundering standards (via mutual evaluations), the APG group and the FATF share methodologies, research and best practises with FIUs and relevant authorities to identify money laundering risks and vulnerabilities.

If implemented fully, the FATF recommendations are designed to protect the economy from the threats of money laundering, financing of terrorism and proliferation, inclusive of the money laundering risks that would be generated from the illegal sale of wildlife products.

National Legal Frameworks

Of the countries studied, all four consider wildlife trafficking to be a predicate offense either directly or by inference (ASEAN-WEN, Freeland, 2016[96]). All of the countries have robust laws and penalties to tackle money laundering. For example, Singapore's maximum term of imprisonment for money laundering is over five times longer than the maximum term of two years for illegal wildlife trade:

Table 6.1. Relevant institutions, laws and penalties to tackle illegal wildlife trade

	Relevant Institution	Money Laundering Predicate Offense (direct or inferred)	National Laws on Anti-Money Laundering	Max Fine for person ($USD or multiple)	Max Penalty	Max Penalty ratio to illegal wildlife trade Max Penalty
Indonesia	Indonesia Financial Transaction Reports Analysis Center (PPATK)	Y	Act No.8/2010 on the prevention and eradication of money laundering Article 3-5	79,470,000	20 years	200%
Singapore	Steering Committee for combating money laundering and terrorist financing[1]	Y	Monetary Authority of Singapore Act (Ch. 186, rev 1999, MoneyLenders (prevention of money laundering and financing of terrorism rules 2009, 2008 Section 11 Corruption, Drug Trafficking and other serious Crimes Act, Chapter 65A, 1992	369,823	10 years	500%
Thailand	Thailand Anti-Money Laundering Offices (AMLO)	Y	Anti-money laundering Act B.E. 2542 (1999) as amended to Anti-Money Laundering Act (No. 4) VE 2556 (2013)	6,105	10 years	142%
Viet Nam	Viet Nam Anti-Money Laundering Department (VAMLD)	Y	Law on Prevention and Fighting against money laundering No. 07/2012/QH13 Article 35 Penal Code 1999, Article 251	3 x value seized	15 years	214%

Source: (ASEAN-WEN, Freeland, 2016[96]).

As the table above has shown, the legal framework for tackling money laundering with illegal wildlife trade as the predicate offense is relatively robust. However, the effectiveness of the laws and measures taken is drawn into question by several institutional gaps reported, notably in the investigation and prosecution of the numerous trafficking cases. As the section below details, it appears that a link between wildlife crime and proceeds of crime and money laundering is not being made.

Assessing Implementation of Anti-Money Laundering

Several of the forty FATF Recommendations are relevant to tackling and enforcing the predicate offense of illegal wildlife trade. For example, the first FATF recommendation calls for a "risk-based approach to money laundering" (FATF, 2012[162]). Recommendation one explains that countries should have a good understanding of what sectors are most vulnerable to money laundering risks. If wildlife crime is understood to be a prominent form of criminality which generate large amounts of proceeds of crime, common responses to wildlife crime should therefore include financial investigations. However, as demonstrated in the interviews with relevant officials and experts, there is no common response to wildlife crime that involves money laundering of proceeds of crime investigations.

FATF Recommendation two calls for cooperation and coordination between relevant national authorities to exchange information through frameworks of co-operation to include parallel money laundering investigations (FATF, 2012[162]). For wildlife crime, such co-ordination might take place between the relevant investigating authority (CITES or Police) and the FIU. Furthermore, recommendations 36-40 focus on international co-ordination, stating for example that FIUs in each country should have in place relevant information sharing arrangements with international counterparts and joint training and learning programmes. For instance, FATF Recommendations 37 and 38 call for the use mutual legal assistance treaties (MLAT) to facilitate the exchange of information and requests for asset seizure and forfeiture (FATF, 2012[162]). Technical compliance with these recommendations is often a pre-requisite to tackling money laundering for the crime in question, however it is not sufficient to address the effectiveness. Indeed, in the case of wildlife crime, with the exception of Thailand, there have been no notable applications of mutual legal assistance for the exchange of financial data, despite the legal groundwork permitting these exchanges.

The APG has held consultations and conducted research on money laundering aspects of illegal wildlife trade. From these, a series of results have emerged that indicate where the status of illegal wildlife trade stands within the region and among other governments. In a recent joint APG and UNODC report summarizing 45 jurisdictions surveyed (APG and non-APG), 86% responded that they were affected by wildlife crime, however over 71% did not consider illegal wildlife trade to be a serious money laundering threat. Furthermore, only 26% of the 45 countries reported any financial investigation into wildlife crimes at all, with less than 1% of all wildlife cases leading to any money laundering investigation, charges or prosecution. Nearly 80% reported that FIUs do not feature on wildlife multi-agency task forces (or WENs) (UNODC/APG, 2017[163]).

The APG's findings are echoed in the research and primary information collection conducted during the OECD surveys across the four focus countries. For instance, Thailand and Indonesia have specifically included FIUs in their multi-agency task forces whereas Viet Nam and Singapore have not (Indonesia PPATK, 2018[56]) (Thailand AMLO, 2018[71]). Thailand is also the sole country to have reported the involvement of its anti-money laundering offices in the investigation, asset seizure and forfeiture of proceeds of crime related to illegal wildlife trade cases. The below case highlights one such recent success, in addition to providing clear evidence of the corruption and money-laundering nexus in wildlife crime:

Box 6.1. Thailand Anti-Money Laundering Case

In 2011, a Thai national was arrested in South Africa for arranging the illegal poaching and importing of rhino horns from South Africa into Thailand. This was done obtaining false licenses for "hunts" in order to kill 24 rhinos over a period of two years through a corrupt network of officials in South Africa who sold permits to kill the endangered rhinos in "hunts". To justify poaching incidents as "hunts" by foreign nationals (which are legal under South African Law), the suspect hired Thai prostitutes in South Africa to pose next to the illegally killed animals. To conduct the joint-investigation, the Thailand AMLO co-ordinated closely and exchanged financial information on bank accounts, properties and contacts with the South African counterparts. According to the investigation from the Thai AMLO, money from proceeds of sale in a Laos based company was wired from the suspect's wife into his accounts (Thailand AMLO, 2018[71]). The smugglers working for the suspect bribed the police officers and customs in Thailand. Smugglers bribed the customs official was paid to ensure that the goods avoided scanner checks upon arrival, and the police officers were paid to escort the suitcases through the airport checkpoints (Freeland, 2018[94]) (Thailand AMLO, 2018[71]). Thanks to the joint investigation, the AMLO seized a number of vehicles, bank accounts and several properties. The suspect is now serving a 40-year jail term in South Africa.

Capacity and Prioritisation Gaps for Money Laundering Investigations for Wildlife Crime

In Thailand, the OECD found two reported investigations involving money laundering charges (one of which is cited in the section above). The exceptional use of Thailand AMLO for the investigation and prosecution of transnational illegal wildlife trade is an example of how such investigations can assist in the dismantling of syndicates. The AMLO case above could also be used for future reference as a good practise guidance for future investigations. Nevertheless, this case remains an exceptional instance of a money laundering investigation related to illegal wildlife trade. Evidence collected by OECD on the seizures of illegal wildlife trade and recent arrests in Thailand throughout the interviews suggests that the vast majority of cases and large-scale seizures do not involve parallel money-laundering investigations.

In Indonesia, the PPATK FIU is included in the "multi-door" inter-agency task force to tackle wildlife crime; however, the nation's FIU has not yet assisted in the investigation or prosecution of money laundering for illegal wildlife trade. Technical gaps and prioritisation of illegal wildlife trade remain the two main obstacles: According to respondents, police must lay charges within two months of arrest whereas the length of time required to collect evidence from domestic and foreign transactions (often through requests to FIU counterparts and institutions abroad) can take substantially longer. In addition to technical barriers, investigators also noted that PPATK is not a standalone investigative body. Therefore, the PPATK must defer to the authority of police to select and conduct investigations. Investigators familiar with the issue also noted that illegal wildlife trade is not a high-level priority for the Indonesia National Police and other relevant administrations that enlist the PPATK to provide investigatory support. For example, the national police most often directs PPATK to focus its resources on major crimes, such as government corruption cases, drug offenses, and tax crimes (Indonesia PPATK, 2018[56]).

The issue of illegal wildlife trade also remains a lesser-known financial crime, and one that appears to be "flying under the radar" with less high-level political support. According to several respondents, the perception among relevant agencies is that wildlife crimes involve smaller sums from illegal wildlife trade transactions (Indonesia PPATK, 2018[56]). Even in the case of large-scale, multi-million dollar seizures, money-laundering investigations were not undertaken. Experts also noted that there is little knowledge of the modus operandi and practises in the financial system for wildlife crimes: wildlife traffickers are still widely perceived to work through cash transactions in small sums, or through money couriers (Indonesia PPATK, 2018[56]). Other respondents noted that the reasons why money laundering is not investigated may also be due to lack of precedent, and the low relative recognition given to this issue among political decision makers (in contrast to logging, for example) (NG-2, 2018[45]).

Perceptions of wildlife crime in Indonesia as a smaller scale financial crime contrast with the perceptions and prioritisation of illegal logging crimes in Indonesia. The latter is recognized as a large multi-million dollar scheme with severe environmental impacts and clear economic damages. The PPATK has been actively involved in several high-level money laundering investigations tackling logging crimes. The case featured below highlights the capabilities of anti-money laundering investigations in prosecuting one such case and highlights how the tracing of assets and multi-agency co-ordination can also assist in tackling the underlying corruption that facilitates environmental crimes:

Box 6.2. Indonesia Money Laundering Investigations for Illegal Logging Cases

In 2014, the supreme court of Indonesia charged a West Papuan police officer with corruption, environmental crimes and money laundering crimes related to illegal logging. The Police officer in question had sold and exported wood illegally cut from forests in Indonesia to destination markets in China, Europe, Australia and the United States. Upon arrest, PPATK investigations revealed that over USD $127 million had passed through connected bank accounts in the years of this scheme, and the investigation unveiled a network of assets, as well as payments for bribery and corruption. In all, PPATK froze 60 bank accounts connected to the suspect in addition to barges, fuel stocks and containers belonging to the company of the suspect. Asset seizure included some 80 containers full of logs destined for export at the time of the arrest (Jakarta Post, 2013[167]).

Upon conviction, the suspect was found guilty of money laundering under the Money Laundering Law No. 25/2003 and No. 8/2010 and sentenced to 15 years in prison and a fine of USD $342,000.

The case in question also revealed the strong corruption-money laundering nexus as well. The convicted person detailed a series of payments and transactions to a number of senior police and state officials over the years and, during the sentence served, the convicted person paid off police and prison officials to leave the prison and remain free for several months at a time (EIA, 2016[168]).

The corruption and money-laundering nexus has been highlighted in the above case of illegal logging schemes. Other cases have documented higher-level political interference relating to logging crimes that have involved politically exposed persons and high-level officials handling millions in proceeds of crime (EIA, 2017[169]). However, in the case of money laundering for wildlife crime, the OECD study did not find any strong evidence suggesting that political pressures from politically exposed persons is preventing parallel investigations. Instead, it appears that there are simply few to none of the already scarce resources within FIUs dedicated to wildlife crimes. This may be due to the perception that this is a labour intensive process that is relatively lower impact than other environmental crimes. However, this does not preclude the involvement of high-level corruption in the illegal wildlife trade chain. The OECD's research can only highlight a lack of knowledge around this particular topic with more immediate and obvious causes, such as lack of awareness of the economic impact from wildlife crime.

Public-Private Co-operation to identify Money Laundering

Financial institutions play a vital role in the exchange of data and information to assist FIUs with identifying high-risk activities that suggest money laundering has taken place. The use of suspicious transaction reports (STRs) are a pillar of the anti-money laundering regimes, and represents a compliance mechanism that enlists the expertise and abilities of banks to detect instances of money changing hands. Banks and financial institutions also use 'Know Your Customer' (KYC) approaches to mitigate high-risk clients, criminal activities and fraudulent users[2]. These practises are mutually beneficial as they also offer the bank cover for high-risk, criminal activities (World Bank, 2006[170]).

STRs and KYC guidelines can assist authorities in identifying high-risk transactions specific to illegal wildlife trade. To this end, in 2018, a number of private sector actors and the United Kingdom Based Royal Foundation launched the *Financial Task Force for Wildlife Crimes* under its United for Wildlife Project to assist with the effort in identifying high-risk activities and developing typologies for money laundering for wildlife crime. The mission of the Financial Task Force also involves raising awareness of how illegal wildlife trade is facilitated by illicit financial flows, providing training to identify suspicious activities, providing intelligence to government bodies and offering policy guidance and support to governments. The financial task force has 39 financial institution signatories.

From a regional perspective, a number of important steps remain to effective implementation of this private-public institution. First, the Task Force does not yet include strong buy-in from Southeast Asian financial institutions (to-date, only three signatory banks are located in Southeast Asia -two in Singapore and one in Viet Nam). The relatively minor participation of financial institutions from Southeast Asia suggests insufficient uptake of this initiative among the major source of illegal wildlife trade illicit financial flows. Furthermore, in order to operate within the region this Task Force will require active participation from FIUs who can offer typologies, suspicious transaction reports, and respond with investigations into the "red-flags" that are raised by the members of this Task Force.

The Financial Task Force hints at the role of public-private engagement in countering money laundering that finances illegal wildlife trade and the corruption that facilitates it. It remains however clear that further uptake is necessary among banks in the Southeast Asian region to work more effectively against illicit financial flows in the region.

Conclusion

The findings from this chapter have shown that that there is no consistent record of financial investigations for money laundering or proceeds of crime in illegal wildlife trade investigations and prosecutions in the focus countries. This finding points to a substantial rift between calls from the international community for a "follow the money approach" to wildlife crime, and the reality in countries most-affected by the illegal wildlife trade. Of the four focus countries, half of all FIUs have a specified role in multi-agency strategies, and only one country (Thailand) has actively employed financial investigations to aid in the investigation and prosecution of wildlife crimes.

Despite the consideration that illegal wildlife trade and the antecedent crimes (such as smuggling) are considered predicate offenses, responses from FIUs and past research indicates that this crime has a relatively lower ranking of priority in comparison to other offenses. Indeed, financial crimes and money laundering from high-level corruption cases and other transnational organized crimes (including logging and forestry crimes) garner more attention than wildlife crimes in Southeast Asia. This is in part due to the nature of wildlife crimes.

The findings from this chapter point towards a greater need to focus resources on financial crime as a component of any wildlife trafficking investigation. Without adequate sanctions in place, such as asset identification, seizure and forfeitures, the crimes from illegal wildlife trade will remain low-risk and high-reward.

References

ASEAN-WEN, Freeland (2016), *ASEAN Handbook on Legal Cooperation to Combat Illegal Wildlife Trade*. [10]

EIA (2017), *Repeat Offender: Vietnam's persistent trade in illegal timber www.eia-international.org EIA US*, Environmental Investigation Agency, http://www.eia-international.org (accessed on 29 April 2019). [17]

EIA (2016), *On-the-run timber crime cop surrenders*, EIA, https://eia-international.org/hes-gone-again-jailed-timber-crime-cop-on-the-run/ (accessed on 15 January 2019). [16]

FATF (2019), *Asia/Pacific Group on Money Laundering (APG)*, http://www.fatf-gafi.org/pages/asiapacificgrouponmoneylaunderingapg.html. [8]

FATF (2019), *FATF Standards*. [9]

FATF (2012), *FATF Recommendations.* [3]

Freeland (2018), *Interviews with Freeland (multiple), Bangkok Thailand, July 2018.* [13]

Haenlein, C. and T. Keatinge (2017), *Follow the Money Using Financial Investigation to Combat Wildlife Crime*, http://www.rusi.org (accessed on 14 January 2019). [6]

Indonesia PPATK (2018), *Interview with Indonesia Financial Transactions Reports and Analysis Center (PPATK), October 19, 2018.* [11]

Jakarta Post (2013), *Papua cop with fat bank accounts faces legal charges*, Jakarta Post, https://www.thejakartapost.com/news/2013/05/17/papua-cop-with-fat-bank-accounts-faces-legal-charges.html (accessed on 15 January 2019). [15]

Nellemann; et al (2016), *The Rise of Environmental Crime – A Growing Threat to Natural Resources, Peace, Development and Security*, Norwegian Center for Global Analyses. [1]

NG-2 (2018), *Interview with Non-governmental organisation 2, Indonesia, October 17, 2018.* [14]

OECD (2019), *Money laundering - OECD*, https://www.oecd.org/cleangovbiz/toolkit/moneylaundering.htm (accessed on 14 January 2019). [2]

OECD (2018), *Strengthening Governance and Reducing Corruption Risks to Tackle Illegal Wildlife Trade: Lessons from East and Southern Africa*, Illicit Trade, OECD Publishing, Paris, https://dx.doi.org/10.1787/9789264306509-en. [4]

OECD (2016), "Illicit Trade: Converging Criminal Networks", *OECD Reviews of Risk Management Policies*, http://dx.doi.org/10.1787/9789264251847-en. [7]

Thailand AMLO (2018), *Interview with Thailand Anti-Money Laundering Authority, Bangkok, Thailand, July 5, 2018.* [12]

UNODC/APG (2017), *Enhanging the Detection, Investigation and Disruption of Illcit Financial Flows from Wildlife Crime.* [5]

World Bank (2006), *Reference Guide to Anti-Money Laundering and Combating the Financing of Terrorism Second Edition and Supplement on Special Recommendation IX*, http://siteresources.worldbank.org/EXTAML/Resources/396511-1146581427871/Reference_Guide_AMLCFT_2ndSupplement.pdf (accessed on 15 January 2019). [18]

Notes

[1] Steering committee comprising the Permanent Secretary of the Ministry of Home Affairs, Permanent Secretary of the Ministry of Finance and Managing Director of the Monetary Authority of Singapore.

[2] "Such profiles would include standard risk indicators such as personal background, country of origin, possession of a public or high profile position, linked accounts, and type and nature of business activity"

Annex A. OECD Structured Interview Questionnaire

Wildlife Crime: Research Questions

The OECD is presently conducting a series of studies on Governance Frameworks to Counter Illegal Wildlife Trade (IWT). There are numerous factors that facilitate illegal wildlife trade. Governance gaps, legislative frameworks and other institutional frameworks can create loopholes that are then exploited for nefarious purposes that lead to the decimation of ecological resources. Corruption is also often cited as a major enabling factor in wildlife trafficking. Defined by Transparency International as abuse of entrusted power for private gain, corruption can facilitate wildlife trafficking throughout the supply chain, assuming a range of different forms and involving a range of different actors at each stage. The OECD Recommendation for Public Integrity provides a comprehensive framework for framing a systemic approach to public integrity, developing a culture of public integrity and enabling accountability. The issue of corruption also pervades the wildlife crime area, with a number of policy issues, and possible knowledge gaps around the wildlife crime–corruption nexus.

The questionnaire below has been elaborated to guide primary data collection on the linkages between governance gaps, such as institutional arrangements, legislative gaps and corruption that enable the illegal wildlife at transit and destination in Southeast Asia. Five core research questions are identified below, with a series of more specific questions elaborated in relation to each. While not all questions will be relevant to all interviewees, they provide a general framework to conduct the interviews. Certain sections can be explored in greater detail than others on the basis of the knowledge and experience of the particular interviewee.

National Conservation Authorities, National Police

In your view, what gaps allows the illicit sourcing of illegal wildlife trade in your country (hunting, illegal/fake captive breeding, farm, etc.)

- What species are being sourced from the economy, and which are subject to the biggest illicit activity?
- Are there legal or regulatory gaps in the current framework that must be addressed?
- Is the system for allocating permits, hunting concessions, and licenses fair and transparent? Are there credible allegations of the system being abused and, if yes, by whom and in what way(s)?

Corruption and sourcing of illegal wildlife trade

- Are there credible allegations of corruption among park or police officers entrusted with the protection of these parks? Or from the administrative officials in charge of issuing CITES permits? From among the types of corrupt conduct listed below, which are the most prevalent?
    - Allowing import of illegal wildlife trade into the country without proper verification;
    - Assisting poachers;
    - Falsification of hunting permits and/or CITES documentation, or selling documentation to poachers;
    - Allowing unlawful hunting trips;
    - Neglecting to patrol a given area;
    - Failing to apprehend the poachers or releasing them after arrest;
    - Making deliberate mistakes in the paperwork so as to impede prosecution;
    - Tipping-off hunters on upcoming patrols or the location of protected species;
    - Returning or selling seized wildlife products and/or ammunition to poachers; or;
    - Directly taking part in poaching.
- Is there evidence that corruption within the private sector facilitates the illicit sourcing of wildlife products?
- Are there credible allegations of corruption in prosecution or courts? If yes, do these have any effect on the prosecution of suspected poachers and/or traffickers? From among the types of corrupt conduct listed below, which are the most prevalent:
    - Dropping cases for improper reasons;
    - Delaying cases;
    - Losing or destroying evidence;
    - Improperly acquitting traffickers;
    - Handing down unduly lenient sentences; or
    - Failing to ensure that convicted poachers and/or traffickers serve their sentences.

Gaps that enable illegal wildlife trade products to circulate (working and sale) within the economy

- What products are processed and/or sold within the domestic economy?
- What gaps in laws and practises allow for illegal wildlife trade products to circulate within the economy?
  - Is this a legal gap or an enforcement gap, or both?
- What capabilities are missing to stop the processing of illegal wildlife trade products in the economy?
- What is the role of electronic commerce and small shipments for the sale of illegal wildlife trade products?
- Is there a "Legal" supply chain of products, and if so, how do illicit goods find their way into this supply chain?
- Are there credible allegations that foreigners, or officials from different countries are engaged in the transport or sale of illegal wildlife products? If yes, how widespread is the phenomenon? From which countries? Are there any states whose diplomats are known to engage in such misconduct on a regular basis?

Corruption and the circulation of illegal wildlife trade products within the economy

- Are there credible allegations of corruption among local public officials that allows the sale of illegal wildlife trade products?
  - Knowingly allowing the sale of illicit wildlife products;
  - Purposely neglecting to inspect paperwork;
  - Directly engaged in the stocking and sale of the products; or
  - Helping to forge the necessary paperwork (CITES permits).

Responses to illegal wildlife trade related crimes

- Is the illegal wildlife trade highlighted as a priority or a part of your organisation's strategic objectives or your organisation's contribution to a national illegal wildlife trade plan?
  - If yes, do you have this report available for public viewing?
  - Does this report also involve anti-corruption measures?
- What actions are taken and by whom to **investigate** wildlife crimes in (your) government organisation?
- Do you have multi-agency task-forces to counter illegal wildlife trade?
  - Which agencies are part of this task force?
  - Is there domestic coordination between wildlife management authorities and authorities with anti-corruption responsibilities such as anti-corruption commissions, law enforcement agencies, financial intelligence units, and judicial authorities?
- Is there international coordination between your administration and others for investigation and prosecution of illegal wildlife trade crimes?
- How are corruption charges addressed?
  - Referred to internal disciplinary hearings and internal corrective actions

  - Referred to external (anti-corruption authorities) for corruption charges
  - Other.
- What measures are in place to prevent the abuse of authority from officers? What best practises function best in preventing abuse? What challenges remain?
  - Is there a system for staff rotation in place?
  - Using operational data to identify trends and patterns that may be indicative of integrity issues?
  - Reinforce management supervision, segregation of duties, and staff rotation in relation with positions that are more vulnerable to corruption and other integrity risks;
  - automated risk management systems indicating what kind of physical examinations or documents checks must be done for each type of cargo based
- What mechanisms are there for whistle-blowing among officials?
- Are the capacities adequate within your administration (awareness, training, and prioritisation) to address illegal wildlife trade? What capacities need to be developed further?
- Overall, do you think current measures to tackle corruption linked to wildlife trafficking are effective? What is missing from the current set of policy tools that would ensure that corruption is properly identified and dealt with in the most effective way possible by law enforcement agencies and justice authorities?
- Please highlight any initiatives that you consider to be best practices.

Customs and Border Police (Import/Export)

What Gaps allow the illegal import of Wildlife products?

- Has there been a considerable change in the number of seizures of illegal wildlife trade products? Are you able to share any data on this?
- What are the biggest hot-spots for illegal wildlife trade into the country? Does this differ by species?
- What are the gaps that are exploited by traffickers to import illegal wildlife trade? Are there legal loopholes or regulatory ones that allow this?
- Who are the main actors involved in the illegal import or illegal wildlife trade products?
- What is known about the involvement of certain private transportation companies in wildlife trafficking? Are shipments of illegal wildlife trade mixed with other types of commodities?

What Gaps allow the illegal export of Wildlife products?

- Has there been a considerable change in the number of seizures of illegal wildlife trade products that are leaving the country? Are you able to share any data on this?
  - What are the biggest hot-spots for the export of illegal wildlife trade products?
  - What are the destination spots for the export of illegal wildlife trade products?
- Are there legal loopholes or regulatory gaps that allow for the lawful export of illegal wildlife trade products?
- Who are the main actors involved in the illegal import or illegal wildlife trade products?

- What is known about the involvement of certain private transportation companies in wildlife trafficking? Are shipments of illegal wildlife trade mixed with other types of commodities?

Evidence of Corruption and Import of illegal wildlife trade products

- Are there credible allegations of corruption among border control officers?
- Are there allegations of corruption among other officials at airports and land and sea ports? Which are the most prevalent?
  - Knowingly letting through shipments that contain illicit wildlife products;
  - Purposely neglecting to inspect shipments and/or paperwork;
  - Assisting traffickers in evading arrest and removing seizures;
  - Helping traffickers forge the necessary paperwork;
  - Forgery or falsification of CITES permits; or
  - On a number of factors, and through which officials should record the checks that have been carried out as well as their result.
- If there is evidence of corruption or collusion with traffickers? Does it take the form of petty corruption by employees or are the company's managers or owners thought to be complicit.
- Are there transportation companies known to be involved in wildlife trafficking that have links to senior public officials or politicians?

Evidence of Corruption and Export of illegal wildlife trade products

- Are there credible allegations of corruption among border control officers?
- Are there allegations of corruption among other officials at airports and land and sea ports? Which are the most prevalent?
  - Knowingly letting through shipments that contain illicit wildlife products;
  - Purposely neglecting to inspect shipments and/or paperwork;
  - Assisting traffickers in evading arrest and removing seizures;
  - Helping traffickers forge the necessary paperwork; or
  - Forgery or falsification of CITES permits.
- If there is evidence of corruption or collusion with traffickers? Does it take the form of petty corruption by employees or are the company's managers or owners thought to be complicit.
- Are there transportation companies known to be involved in wildlife trafficking that have links to senior public officials or politicians?

Responses to illegal wildlife trade related crimes

- Is the illegal wildlife trade highlighted as a priority or a part of your organisation's strategic objectives or your organisation's contribution to a national illegal wildlife trade plan?
  - If yes, do you have this report available for public viewing?
  - Does this report also involve anti-corruption measures?
- What actions are taken and by whom to **investigate** wildlife crimes in (your) government organisation?

- Do you have multi-agency task-forces to counter illegal wildlife trade?
  - Which agencies are part of this task force?
  - Is there domestic coordination between wildlife management authorities and authorities with anti-corruption responsibilities such as anti-corruption commissions, law enforcement agencies, financial intelligence units, and judicial authorities?
- Is there international coordination between your administration and others for investigation and prosecution of illegal wildlife trade crimes?
- How are corruption charges addressed?
  - Referred to internal disciplinary hearings and internal corrective actions
  - Referred to external (anti-corruption authorities) for corruption charges
  - Other.
- What measures are in place to prevent the abuse of authority from customs officers and others? What best practises function best in preventing abuse? What challenges remain?
  - Is there a system for staff rotation in place?
  - Using operational data to identify trends and patterns that may be indicative of integrity issues?
  - Reinforce management supervision, segregation of duties, and staff rotation in relation with positions that are more vulnerable to corruption and other integrity risks?
  - Automated risk management systems indicating what kind of physical examinations or documents checks must be done for each type of cargo based
- What mechanisms are there for whistle-blowing among officials?
- Are the capacities adequate within your administration (awareness, training, and prioritisation) to address illegal wildlife trade? What capacities need to be developed further?
- Overall, do you think current measures to tackle corruption linked to wildlife trafficking are effective? What is missing from the current set of policy tools that would ensure that corruption is properly identified and dealt with in the most effective way possible by law enforcement agencies and justice authorities?
- Please highlight any initiatives that you consider to be best practices.

Anti-Corruption Authorities and illegal wildlife trade

Evidence

- Has your country undertaken risk assessments to identify corruption risks in public institutions? Does this assessment include institutions like wildlife management and trade in wildlife and wildlife products, including customs, maritime ports and airports, as well as in relation to the processes your country uses in the import and export of wildlife and wildlife products?
- Has your country developed and disseminated evidence and typologies on how corruption drives illegal trade in wildlife and wildlife products?
  - Has your country taken any steps to collect, analyse and use data on cases of corruption related to illegal trade in wildlife and wildlife products, as well as to

review progress and conduct regular mappings of relevant cases and to make this information accessible to the public? If so, are you able to share this data?

- Who are the actors typically involved in corruption that facilitates poaching and wildlife trafficking within each of the following spheres?
    - Political
    - Judicial
    - Law enforcement
    - Military
- Are storage rooms for illegal wildlife trade seizures vulnerable to corruption (theft and re-sale of stockpiles)
- Is corruption both high-level and low-level? Are low-level officials such as park rangers, rank-and-file police officers or local judges subject to pressure from their superiors if they seek to investigate or sanction poaching and wildlife trafficking?
- Who are the private-sector actors typically involved in corruption that facilitates poaching and wildlife trafficking? Does it take the form of petty corruption by employees or are the company's managers or owners thought to be complicit?
- What is known about the involvement of organised crime in wildlife trafficking and the mechanics through which organised crime groups facilitate corruption? Is corruption mostly opportunistic, e.g. poachers pay off park rangers or police officers if caught, or do stable corrupt relationships exist between traffickers and public officials?
- Do organised crime groups tend to rely on the expertise of 'fixers' known to have good connections among wildlife officials and law enforcement agencies, so as to communicate indirectly?

Causes and motivations for Corruption

- Apart from economic gain, what other incentives are there for public officials to engage in wrongdoing (e.g. orders from superiors, family loyalties etc.)? How significant are these compared to economic gain?
- Is the recruitment of public officials fair and transparent? Are bribes paid in return for appointments? Does the answer differ depending on the category of public officials, such as park rangers, customs officers, police officers, prosecutors, judges and civil servants?
- Do customs and police officers benefit from sufficient professional training to complete their daily duties?
- What are the consequences of engagement in corruption? Are they sufficiently serious to act as a deterrent?

Institutional responses to Corruption

- What are the functions and powers of the anti-corruption agency for tackling wildlife trafficking explicitly?
- Are the relevant public officials subject to a code of ethics? If yes, is it binding and how is it enforced? Do they receive training on ethics and anti-corruption?
- Do you have multi-agency task-forces to counter illegal wildlife trade and more specifically to reduce corruption risks?

  - Is there domestic coordination between authorities with anti-corruption responsibilities and wildlife management authorities (e.g. including anti-corruption commissions, law enforcement agencies, financial intelligence units, and judicial authorities)?
- What mechanisms are there for whistle-blowing among officials? Are whistle-blowers legally protected from retaliation by their superiors and are these protections effective in practice? How are the allegations of corruption and/or other wrongdoing investigated and sanctioned?
- Are there laws in place to prevent conflicts of interest, e.g. in relation to the allocation of hunting concessions? How are they monitored and enforced?
- Do anti-corruption agencies regularly cooperate with the authorities in charge of combatting wildlife crime and, if so, how?
- Are law enforcement agencies that deal with wildlife crime and/or corruption well-staffed and do they receive sufficient resources? Are they free from political interference?
- What measures are in place to ensure the competence and integrity of the judiciary? How is potential judicial misconduct investigated and sanctioned? Are the mechanisms of judicial accountability used fairly, impartially and effectively?

Corruption Responses and Strategies

- Is there a national strategy or action plan to combat corruption?
  - If yes, has the administration / country taken any steps to promote the incorporation of anti-corruption measures into the work of wildlife enforcement?
  - Does your country have measures to oblige or encourage public organizations to implement the national anti-corruption policies and/or strategies or their own independent anti-corruption measures?
  - Are there incentives for public organizations for its good performances in implementing the anti-corruption measures?
- What actions are taken and by whom to **investigate** internal corruption in (your) government organisation?
- What actions are taken, and by whom, to **prevent** corruption that facilitate wildlife trafficking?
- What is the role of civil society organisations in addressing corruption relative to illicit wildlife trafficking? How effective are these organisations in this role?
- What has been done in the countries to use international frameworks, such as the UN Convention against Corruption (UNCAC) and the UN Convention against Transnational Organized Crime (UNTOC) to combat corruption in relation to the wildlife trade? This is specifically called for by the recent CITES resolution on anti-corruption.
- Please provide a high-level summary of the most significant anti-corruption measures or initiatives directly linked to, or that can indirectly address, the illegal trade in wildlife and wildlife products, that your country has introduced or implemented? Please highlight any initiatives that you consider to be best practices.
- How is their implementation monitored and what evidence is there of their implementation, nationally and locally?
- Overall, do you think current measures to tackle corruption linked to wildlife trafficking are effective? What is missing from the current set of policy tools that

would ensure that corruption is properly identified and dealt with in the most effective way possible by law enforcement agencies and justice authorities?

Legislation

- Does your country have legislation and regulations to enable the prosecution of corruption linked to the illegal trade in wildlife and wildlife products and to seize and recover assets related thereto? If yes, please list the most relevant legislation or regulations, including specific laws on corruption related to illegal trade in wildlife where they exist. Please include electronic links to legislation.
- Does the country criminalise offences established under the UN Convention against Corruption (UNCAC), namely: active and passive bribery of national and foreign public officials; embezzlement, misappropriation, or other diversion of property by public officials; laundering the proceeds of crime; and the obstruction of justice in relation to corruption?
- Does the country criminalise offences listed in the non-mandatory provisions of the UN Convention against Corruption, namely: active and passive bribery in the private sector; embezzlement of property in the private sector; trading in influence; other abuse of functions for an undue advantage; concealment of the proceeds of corruption crimes; and illicit enrichment (a significant increase in the assets of a public official that he or she cannot reasonably explain in relation to his or her lawful income)?
- Are all public officials required by law to disclose their assets? How is this monitored and enforced?

Investigations and prosecutions

Investigations

- Are investigations into illegal wildlife trade often conducted after a seizure of illegal wildlife trade products? Who is in charge of conducting these investigations?
- Do investigators of illegal wildlife trade crimes have adequate resources and/or training to conduct their duties? Are there specialized investigators for illegal wildlife trade crimes?
- Do law enforcement authorities regularly seek to identify and prosecute related corruption offences when wildlife offences are detected?
- Has your country taken any steps to raise awareness about the relevance of reporting corruption acts related to illegal wildlife trade and wildlife products?

Prosecution

- Has your country identified best practices in the prosecution of corruption cases related to illegal trade in wildlife and wildlife products?
- Are there statistics on the number of corruption prosecutions related to poaching and wildlife trafficking and the types of corruption involved?
- Can prosecutions be brought against private companies or their employees who intentionally or negligently facilitate illicit wildlife trafficking (e.g., transportation companies)? If yes, have any such prosecutions been brought?
- Is evidence stored securely in courts and are detailed inventories kept? Have there been issues in the past with evidence / exhibit control?
- Do the range and type of actors involved vary depending on the type of the commodity?

Annex B. Evaluative Assumptions for Analysing Institutional Capacities to Counter Illegal Wildlife Trade

No set of practises can provide a one-size-fits-all solution to combat the illegal wildlife trade. The desk research, literature review and discussions with relevant experts in law enforcement, do provide a number of good practises that could be tailored to local circumstances. From these good practises, a set of evaluative metrics can be established for the purpose of setting a baseline against which country and regional performance can be measured. The following assumptions are key elements in the analytical assessments for this report:

Assumption: Multi-stakeholder engagement is preferable to unilateral action

In most cases, the involvement of a number of relevant agencies can be considered to be better that the engagement of a single entity. Broadly speaking, multiple agencies have more expertise, more investigative capacities and add more transparency to a given process. Indicators of success are the existence of multi-agency task forces; the number of relevant agencies involved; their use and operationalisation (successful investigations and prosecutions).

Assumption: International Co-operation is more effective in tackling illegal wildlife trade than single-country enforcement

Illegal wildlife trade is facilitated by transnational organized crime. The co-ordination among relevant law enforcement agencies from other countries in the illegal wildlife trade and value chain is necessary to ensure a more comprehensive upstream and downstream investigation into the crimes in question. Performance measurements for this would be the number of reported engagements or joint-operations with international counterparts, and the number of times information exchange pathways have been used for illegal wildlife trade.

Assumption: Prosecuting the wildlife trafficking alone is not as effective as sanctions for which wildlife crime or smuggling is a predicate crime

This assumption is based on the documented fact that wildlife trafficking remains a high-reward low-risk crime. This is based on the knowledge that convictions using specific wildlife trafficking laws are either i) difficult to assure if standalone crimes; or ii) too weak (in sentencing and in financial penalty) to deter criminal acts for illegal wildlife trade. Performance metrics for this would be the number of other ancillary parallel investigations or prosecutions for crimes such as money laundering, corruption, or smuggling that have taken place using other legal frameworks beyond the predicate offense (such as violations of the more narrow wildlife protection laws).

Assumption: A strong legal framework with well-implemented laws is more effective than a set of laws with gaps or overlaps

Criminal organisations and consumers alike are affected by the risk and reward of committing crimes and purchasing illegal wildlife products. This assumption is also based on the principle that *if* there is a way for illegal wildlife trade to appear legal, consumers will prefer to consume in apparent legal channels, and consumption of illegal wildlife trade will increase. Consequently, where legal gaps and loopholes in enforceability of laws exist, there will be more consumption, sales and poaching. Measures and performance metrics would be the number and range of efforts undertaken by governments to close identified or known loopholes, or to act in a way to enforce existing laws (i.e. to move from *de jure* to *de facto).*

Assumption: Anti-corruption measures are an important tool to combat wildlife trafficking

Corruption risks play an important role in the illegal wildlife trade chain. For countries where it is identified as a problem, the involvement of anti-corruption agencies suggests that illegal wildlife trade is taken more seriously and with greater intent to charge offenders with a broader range of crimes. Anti-corruption legislation can enhance deterrence capabilities to prevent the involvement of public officials in illegal wildlife trade crimes. It is difficult to measure performance in absolute terms for anti-corruption efforts. Indicators of success could be: the involvement of anti-corruption agencies in illegal wildlife trade task forces or investigations, the number of anti-corruption cases and convictions, and the use of anti-corruption guidelines in vulnerable agencies can be interpreted as good measures.

Assumption: 'Follow the money' approaches to illegal wildlife trade are an effective tool to counter illegal wildlife trade

Wildlife crime is considered a high reward, low-risk crime. While there are few cases of anti-money laundering or asset seizures and forfeitures relating to wildlife crime, the use of follow the money approaches is useful both for investigative purposes and for the goal of enhancing the weight of penalties: Following the money can help investigators to make connections with transnational criminal groups; asset seizure, and money laundering charges can increase the penalties by increasing the size of fines and sentence lengths. To measure the performance of this, it is necessary to identify the number of cases of illegal wildlife trade that have either engaged relevant financial intelligence authorities or that have included asset seizures or prosecutions for money laundering.

ORGANISATION FOR ECONOMIC CO-OPERATION AND DEVELOPMENT

The OECD is a unique forum where governments work together to address the economic, social and environmental challenges of globalisation. The OECD is also at the forefront of efforts to understand and to help governments respond to new developments and concerns, such as corporate governance, the information economy and the challenges of an ageing population. The Organisation provides a setting where governments can compare policy experiences, seek answers to common problems, identify good practice and work to co-ordinate domestic and international policies.

The OECD member countries are: Australia, Austria, Belgium, Canada, Chile, the Czech Republic, Denmark, Estonia, Finland, France, Germany, Greece, Hungary, Iceland, Ireland, Israel, Italy, Japan, Korea, Latvia, Lithuania, Luxembourg, Mexico, the Netherlands, New Zealand, Norway, Poland, Portugal, the Slovak Republic, Slovenia, Spain, Sweden, Switzerland, Turkey, the United Kingdom and the United States. The European Union takes part in the work of the OECD.

OECD Publishing disseminates widely the results of the Organisation's statistics gathering and research on economic, social and environmental issues, as well as the conventions, guidelines and standards agreed by its members.

OECD PUBLISHING, 2, rue André-Pascal, 75775 PARIS CEDEX 16
ISBN 978-92-64-70887-7 – 2019

www.ingramcontent.com/pod-product-compliance
Lightning Source LLC
LaVergne TN
LVHW081413110826
845149LV00010B/1724

* 9 7 8 9 2 6 4 7 0 8 8 7 7 *